D0447049

Best Buys
in Rare Coins

Best Buys
in Rare Coins

What Expert Dealers and Collectors Advise

Donn Pearlman

Bonus Books, Inc., Chicago

© 1990 by Bonus Books
All rights reserved

Except for appropriate use in critical reviews or works of scholarship, the reproduction or use of this work in any form or by any electronic, mechanical or other means now known or hereafter invented, including photocopying and recording, and in any information storage and retrieval system is forbidden without the written permission of the publisher.

94 93 92 91 90   5 4 3 2 1

Library of Congress Catalog Card Number: 90-84285

International Standard Book Number: 0-933893-92-2

Bonus Books, Inc.
160 East Illinois Street
Chicago, Illinois 60611

Text and cover photos: James A. Simek

All coin photos have been enlarged to show design details.

Printed in the United States of America

To my understanding wife Fran and son Russell, who both knew that even when I finished researching and writing this latest book my office-at-home would still remain, "The Pit."

CONTENTS

ACKNOWLEDGMENTS

Special thanks to the following for their encouragement, suggestions, expertise, and good humor.

The nice folks at Bonus Books, Inc., Chicago, who originally wanted me to write a numismatic book back in the early 1980s, but who first let me write books on broadcasting and baseball cards. Then they quietly munched on antacids until I delivered this book's manuscript four months past the deadline.

Gentleman Jim Simek, an outstanding numismatic photographer, a respected rare coin expert, and best of all, a good friend.

In addition to those people specifically named in this book, the author gratefully thanks the following individuals and organizations for their assistance: The American Numismatic Association, Amos Press and Leonard Albrecht of ANACS, Krause Publications, and Early American Coppers.

CHAPTER ONE

A Busy Person's Guide to Coins and Coin Collecting

"This is not reliable. This is not safe.

This is buyer beware."

-Phoebe Morse-

If you're looking for sure-fire suggestions on how to instantly double or triple your money with rare coins, here is the author's candid, sure-fire advice: Promptly close this book and return it directly to the shelf—do not pass "Go," do not collect $200.

Guaranteed, instant riches will not be found in this book. Frankly, one volume alone can not effectively teach you all the tricks of the trade or provide you with enough background to guarantee you'll always make a quick killing in the numismatic market. To acquire that kind of information requires a decent library and years of experience. It also requires a considerable amount of luck to be in the right place at the right time. Being able to correctly tell the difference between a coin labeled Mint State 64 (MS-64) and a comparable specimen labeled MS-65 can make or save you thousands of dollars.

If you are new to the numismatic marketplace, U.S. coins usually are graded on a numerical scale ranging from 1 to 70, but as you'll quickly discover, confusion over that scale ranges from 1 to 7,000.

A word about rare coin grading: Caution. Another word about rare coin grading: Knowledge. Combine the two and you'll be on steady ground. Because the value of most coins is directly connected to the grade—the condition—you must familiarize yourself with numismatic grading. Learn more than just the terminology. Learn how to grade, how to tell the difference between a coin that is Very Fine and a similar one that is Extremely Fine. Learn the difference between Mint State 64 and 65 because that one point difference can change a price tag by hundreds or even thousands of dollars. Deliberately or unintentionally labeling a MS-64 coin as MS-65 is overgrading. It was a common problem prior to third-party grading service encapsulation, and still a problem even with independent opinions by outside grading services. Now and then, MS-64 coins do get "slabbed" MS-65 much to the thrill of the person who submitted it. Slabs, the hobby's nickname for coins that have been certified and sealed inside special plastic holders, have indeed eliminated many previously common grading complaints, but there are still substantial differences of opinion.

The controversy involving grading U.S. coins has been traced back a century to 1892 by researchers Richard Bagg and James J. Jelinski (*Grading Coins: A Collection of Readings*, Essex Publications, 1977). Obviously, overgrading is certainly not a new problem, or limited to just the United States and U.S. coinage. The best way to begin your study of grading is by reading the first two dozen or so pages of *Official American Numismatic Association (ANA) Grading Standards for United States Coins*, and read the "how to" grading section of either *The Investor's Guide to Coin Trading* or *The Coin Collector's Survival Manual*, both by Scott A. Travers.

Although a coin can be described merely as "uncirculated"—showing no signs of wear—there actually are eleven different designations of Uncirculated ranging from a banged up, nicked up, and scratched Mint State 60 to a flawless, pristine 70. At the 1986 American Numismatic Association convention in Milwaukee, I gave a brief presentation pointing out that with an 11 point Mint State grading scale you have 121 possible different grading combinations for describing the obverse and reverse of any uncirculated coin! The front can be MS-62 while the back can be MS-68, and so on.

Larger coins, such as silver dollars and $20 gold pieces, often are seen with distracting gouges, marks, and other blemishes that were made when the coins jostled against each other when shipped by the mint in big bags. The coin is still uncirculated—no wear—but detracting marks take away from its grade. A mark-free coin that might have graded MS-65 or better, but has been harshly cleaned will get a lower grade because of its "impaired luster." An otherwise blemish free coin also may have a lower value because it was not fully struck, all the design elements are not sharp and well defined. (Try to find a fully struck 1945-S Walking Liberty half dollar.) Even if the weakly struck coin is graded MS-65 it may not bring "65 money." It will sell at a discount compared to other MS-65 pieces with sharper strikes.

Coins that have just the slightest amout of wear are described as AU, About Uncirculated, and depending on the quality are noted as either AU-58, AU-55, or AU-50. Old timers (anyone in the hobby before 1980) may refer to AU-58 coins as "sliders" because a Choice About Uncirculated condition coin often is so nice looking you can slide it past an unsuspecting buyer as Uncirculated.

There are two categories of Extremely Fine coins, XF-45 and 40, and two designations for Very Fine, VF-30 and 20. In the lower grades, you'll find Fine as F-15 and F-12, Very Good as VG-8, Good as G-4, and About Good designated AG-3. Non-collectors may describe a coin as being in "good condition," thinking that's a nice adjective, but in numismatic terms, Good condition actually describes a rather worn coin.

A coin so worn there is virtually no design showing may be listed as B-1, Basal State. Why these confusing numbers of 1 through 70? In the 1958 book, *Penny Whimsy*, author Dr. William H. Sheldon originally related the numbers to the grades and values of early U.S. copper large cents. Dr. Sheldon suggested a system starting with Basal State-1, a barely recognizable coin, up to Mint State-70, a seldom seen, perfect condition specimen with perhaps just a mellowing of its original mint red luster. Today, any similar correlation between a Sheldon number and the value of the coin seems strictly coincidence.

To the dismay and frustration of collectors of early American copper, the "Sheldon Scale" has assumed a different identity, an identity that evolved quickly in the 1980s and seems to have little if any direct correlations to values except that the higher the MS number, the higher the price of the coin. In 1982 there even was an advertisement offering a blank planchet (a metal coin disc before it is struck by the coinage dies) described as "MS-65." Not only that, the planchet was for a British coin, not even a U.S. product!

If you have no intention of learning about grading, about the sharp strike or weakness of design, the color, luster and overall eye appeal of coins, you may as well simply toss $20, $50 and $100 bills at random into the nearest busy street. Accuracy in grading is an absolutely crucial element in getting good value for your money because the true market value of most coins is directly related to the grade of the coins. The age of the coin may not even be much of a factor. Years ago, Chicago area dealer Larry Whitlow had a sign in his store: "The age of a coin is like that of a person. It's the CONDITION that counts."

Fast profits in rare coins usually are possible only for those who have successfully and sometimes painstakingly acquired vital knowledge and skills. Knowledge and skills that help you find an under-priced, scarce variety of a particular coin nestled with otherwise common specimens in a dealer's stock; knowledge and skills to realize when a coin offered for sale has been labeled and priced too conservatively, and knowing you quickly can re-sell it at a higher grade and price; and knowledge and skill to act when attending an auction sale where no one else wants to bid more than $50 for a coin you know is worth at least $200 or $2,000.

No, if you're looking to quickly double or triple your money with coins, try tossing a few quarters into a slot machine. Your odds might be better. Sure, you've probably read advertisements and newsletters proclaiming there are coins that will increase 50, 75 or 100 percent in six months or a year. But, there also are coins that may lose 25 or 50 percent of their value in that same time. Too often, the only sure thing about sure-fire rare coin investing is the fire. You can get burned.

This book looks at coins that slowly and steadily may increase in value, coins that have a track record of performance, coins that have wider appeal than highly-touted, "limited mintage" special issues that usually are accompanied by dubious promises of fast profits. Frequently, the only thing "limited" about "limited issue" coins is the chance for a future profit. This book looks at coins that expert dealers, collectors and investors believe have beauty to the eyes of the beholders and *potential* profits to the owners. These are coins that have built a following over the years, coins that have become popular for their own sake, not just because a few "market makers" are trying to manipulate prices for a few months to attract investors.

You use money virtually every day, but do you ever think about the money itself? You should. Coins were first struck around the mid-seventh century B.C., and coin collecting is one of the oldest hobbies, in a sense, a nearly 3,000-year-old pastime. Look at your own pocket change or paper money, and think about the people, places and events symbolized in the coinage and currency designs. From the first coins of ancient Greece to the latest pieces just off the press, money is history you can hold in your hands. Respected researcher and New Hampshire dealer Q. David Bowers wrote a fascinating, 527-page book about U.S. history as seen through the country's coins and currency, *The History of United States Coinage—As Illustrated by the Garrett Collection*. That famous collection was assembled in the nineteenth and early twentieth centuries by the railroad magnate family of T. Harrison Garrett. It eventually was acquired by the Johns Hopkins University, Baltimore, and sold in a series of auctions from 1979 to 1981 by Bowers & Ruddy Galleries (now Bowers & Merena, Wolfeboro, New Hampshire) for a total of $25,235,360. At the time, it set the record for the largest amount of money realized for any collection of fine art property auctioned in America.

Just as coin designs have changed over the decades and centuries, the rare coin market in the United States has changed drastically since the days—not that long ago—when collectors casually plugged pocket change into blue folders or brown albums. Now, there are the "collector" coins and "investor" coins. Often, the same kind of coin can be collector or investor, usually depending on its condition. The higher the grade, the higher the value. Sometimes the value can be unbelievably higher. A well-worn and quite common 1907 Indian Head cent easily can be purchased for well under one dollar, but a dazzling, spotless, bright red colored specimen sold at auction in January 1990 for $33,000 (including a 10 percent buyer's fee). Both the beat up cent and its pristine cousin have the same face value, the same historical value, and virtually the same intrinsic copper metal value, but the lure of a "finest known" obviously fascinated someone with a heavy checkbook, and the superb quality coin sold for a record-setting price. Since the late 1970s, there has been a two-tier numismatic market, "collector" coins versus "investor" coins; now the market has entered the era of the "super-grade" investor coins. Despite the hype and hoopla over super prices for super-grade coins, there is room for everyone. You do not need deep pockets to enjoy rare coins and currency.

New York dealer and rare coin investment newsletter publisher Maurice Rosen uses his wristwatch as an analogy. He is perfectly happy with his "moderately priced" watch that accurately tells time and contains a calculator, a stop-watch, and even a telephone number data bank. While others may pay thousands of dollars for a Rolex or a Patek Philippe watch, Rosen's choice is a $30 Casio. "The marketplace is large enough to accommodate all tastes . . . from an $8 bottle of wine to someone's $800 bottle. From a Mint State 63 coin costing $45 to an MS-67 of the same issue at $2,600," he explains.

A 1989 survey of readers of the popular weekly hobby newspaper *Numismatic News* indicated that 55 percent of the respondents began collecting coins before the age of eighteen. Thirty-nine percent indicated they are rare coin "investors." Yet, most *collectors* hope they'll make a profit on their purchases when they eventually sell their coins. So, in a way, most coin collectors also are investors. But that word, investment, gnaws at many collectors who conjure visions of custom-made, pin-striped suits, complicated financial charts tracking prices of specific coins or sets, and the indifferent buying and selling of beloved, historic numismatic specimens as though they merely were dull shares of stock or boxcars of grain. If you want to invest in rare coins, at least become that hybrid known as a collector-investor. It can be the best of both worlds, the joy of feeling the pride of ownership and the happiness of knowing that your acquisitions have appreciated in value while you have been appreciating them for their own sake.

Three words describe many of the coin market's recent drastic changes: "Slabs" and "Wall Street." Slab is the hobby's vogue term for the plastic holders into which private grading services seal individual coins after they have been independently evaluated for authenticity and their condition —state of preservation—determined. You'll hear the phrases, "I'm sending this coin to be slabbed," or "That dealer sells only slabs, no raw (unslabbed) coins." The term, slab, is a heck of a lot easier to say than "encapsulated numismatic product."

David Hall, the Sultan of Slabs, the Prince of Plastic, has been one of the main movers in this important area. An organizer of the highly successful Professional Coin Grading Service (PCGS) in Newport Beach, California, Hall and his colleagues literally changed the way business had been conducted for decades in the United States rare coin market. The February 1986 introduction of PCGS slabs thankfully eliminated some of the guesswork about grading and, therefore, made it easier to estimate a rare coin's value; but slabs also created additional controversies and problems. There are still differences of opinion on whether an ecapsulated (slabbed) coin truly is accurately graded or not. Someone could fill an entire book with case studies of how coins have been submitted to grading services, removed from the slabs and then resubmitted to the same or different grading services, and the coins returned with different grades. Here are two examples from Q. David Bowers.

"A coin appeared in Auction '86 described as AU-50, and after passing through one or more hands, was consigned to an auction sale of ours, where we graded it similarly. The latest buyer sent it to a well-known slabbing service, had it returned marked MS-62, and doubled the price. We were subsequently re-offered the coin, questioned the grade (not first recognizing the coin as one we had owned earlier), and were told: 'What's the difference? Your customer will just read the slab.' Seeking to see if we and the cataloguer of the lot in Auction '86 were a bit confused, we put a piece of tape over the grade on the slab, and passed it around among six professional numismatists, who were not aware of the grade, and asked them what the grade was. The opinions ranged from AU-50 to AU-55, none higher.

"In another instance a client bought a $10 gold coin in one of our sales, sent it to a well-known grading service, and had it returned as 'damaged—cannot be encapsulated.' Failing to see any damage on the coin, he resubmitted it, and the second time around it came back graded ten points higher than listed in our auction catalogue! The point of this is that slabbed coins are fine and dandy, our customers like them a lot, and they are here to stay. However, the role of the professional numismatist is still important, and while investors might want to buy coins sight-unseen and with a devil-may-care attitude, nearly all insiders, old-timers, and discriminating buyers want to take a peek at the coin, evaluate it independently, and be sure they are getting what they pay for."

Used as a noun or a verb, the word "slab" can evoke cries of ecstacy or agony from delighted dealers, investors and veteran collectors. Slabs "have brought standardized grading, improved liquidity, and grading guarantees to the rare coin industry for the first time," proudly and justifiably states a PCGS brochure, adding that third-party certification "has become a revolution heralding a new era of safety and reliability for coin collectors and investors."

A veteran Illinois collector, Hugh Cooper, a member of the American Numismatic Association's Consumer Protection and Education Committee, has a slightly skeptical view: "Slabbing has enabled anonymous klunks to buy and sell coins they may never see. . . . I am strenuously opposed to slabbing on the ground that it leads to market disruption for collectors. I am also, therefore, opposed to investors and speculators because they offend and assault the hobby and its desire to cultivate its own garden."

Despite the opposition, it is apparent that slabs are an integral part of the two-tier numismatic marketplace. More than a dozen private companies and organizations offer grading services, but only three seem to have wide acceptance, PCGS, Numismatic Guarantee Corporation (NGC) in Parsippany, New Jersey, and the American Numismatic Association Certification Service known as ANACS, originally operated by the American Numismatic Association in Colorado Springs, Colorado, and sold to Amos Press of Sidney, Ohio, in the summer of 1990. Even among those three widely accepted slabbing services, there can be a 5 to 20 percent difference in the prices of two identical coins with the same grade but assigned by different grading services. You have to know the market if you are going to play these games.

Mark Borkardt, senior numismatist at Bowers & Merena Galleries explained to readers of the company's newsletter, *Rare Coin Review*:

"Time was, back in 1986 and 1987, when the chances were good that a coin in a slab was better than the typical offering outside of the slab. However, the situation has slipped, and the connoisseur knows well that slabs are not the magical answer to either quality or value at this point. For the uninitiated investor—the buyer who knows nothing at all about coins and doesn't want to know about them—slabs do offer a measure of protection, for there is no doubt that a Morgan dollar in a slab marked MS-63, even if it is dingy, banged up, and not particulaly desirable to a discriminating numismatist, still has a ready market and can be bought and sold at bid and ask levels."

Wall Street entered the marketplace primarily because slabs eliminated so much guesswork and debate about grading, and, therefore, vastly improved the sight-unseen trading of coins. For years, the prominent New York investment company Salomon Brothers annually has indicated rare coins are among the best tangible investments; yet many investors stayed away because of the obstacles involving consistently accurate grading and dealers' profit margins. Slabbing not only reduced the gross and deliberate acts of overgrading (for example, a dealer falsely claiming that an MS-62 coin was MS-65), it also has significantly reduced the Buy and Sell spreads on many commonly traded rare coins, thereby reducing dealers' profit margins.

Elimination of many overgrading problems, lowering profit margins, and improving liquidity were enough for some Wall Street brokerage houses to enter the market. Starting in 1989, Kidder Peabody, and Merrill Lynch (which earlier offered limited partnerships involving ancient coins) began offering tens of millions of dollars in rare coin limited partnerships with many of their coin purchases authenticated, evaluated, and slabbed by third-party grading services to independently provide more accurate establishment of their values as well as greater ease of buying and selling, liquidity. The Kidder Peabody limited partnership, The American Rare Coin Fund L.P., invested $42 million in rare coins during its first nine months of operation. In early 1990, one of the fund's prominent leaders, Hugh Sconyers of Beverly Hills, California, said he expected he would invest another $100 million by the end of the year. However, the rare coin market has picked up a nasty habit found on Wall Street, buying on the rumor and selling on the news.

Whenever there are rumors of some brokerage house even glancing at the numismatic marketplace, action picks up. Prices are bid up on the computerized dealer-to-dealer networks as speculators eagerly anticipate tens of millions of new dollars entering the market. Coin market promoters feed on the rumor frenzy, encouraging potential customers to buy now before prices go even higher. James U. Blanchard III, president of Blanchard and Company, Inc., New Orleans, explains it this way:

"It doesn't take much to move the rare coin market. Compared to other investments like stocks and commodities, the rare coin supply is small and static. This is why it took only a relatively small shift in investor attention to send coin prices soaring in excess of 1,000 percent from 1977 to 1980. And this is why it took only $20 million in new demand in the spring of 1989 to push prices up 100 percent." (That boom was touched off by Merrill Lynch notifying the Securities and Exchange Commission of its proposed rare coin fund.)

These sudden surges prompt some dealers to tout "panic buying." One dealership sent out letters pleading with customers to get in on the "ground floor" of the Wall Street demand for rare coins. "Wouldn't you like to have been in line the day that IBM stock was first offered? Or the first shares of McDonalds?" the advertising pitch declared.

Despite the considerable financial muscle of major brokerage houses, it still can be a thin market, and if there is not the expected demand for rare coins the prices can drop quickly. In April 1989, the *Wall Street Journal* printed a story indicating that Shearson Lehman Hutton might not enter the rare coin market, and the prices for some coins (especially the Saint-Gaudens type $20 gold pieces) plunged by about 30 percent within hours. In March 1990, a rare coin "market maker" who was purchasing items for a Wall Street brokerage house suddenly withdrew his public bids because he thought prices were too high. Trading abruptly halted across the board for many items, and when it resumed, prices were about 30 percent lower than they were twenty-four hours earlier. In both cases, prices eventually went back to their earlier levels. Like the agony and the ecstacy experienced by Chicago Cubs baseball fans, wild gyrations in a period of weeks, days, or hours are part of the territory in much of the "investor" market.

Keith M. Zaner, trends editor of *Coin World,* in a May 2, 1990 column headlined "Volatility Result of Thin Market," reflectively asked: "Are there enough market makers to sufficiently meet the market demands? Periodically, when one, or more, major market maker removes his bids or substantially lowers or raises his bid, it would appear that dramatic price movements take place. Are these price movements a real reflection of the current coin market or are they sporadic false signals?"

Phil Schuyler of Ellesmere Numismatics in Connecticut explained the ballgame this way in his dealership's newsletter, *The Winning Edge*: "Dealers do not control the coin market, they react to it."

Also in the late 1980s the Federal Trade Commission aggressively entered the numismatic marketplace because of suspected fraud among mail-order and telemarketing companies dealing in rare coins. In March 1990, the New England Region FTC Commissioner, Phoebe Morse, told the American Numismatic Association there would be continuing, vigorous prosecution in additional rare coin cases.

"On one hand the coin industry as a whole has in a sense raised the stakes by inviting Wall Street into the market. Essentially the message is: 'This is safe. This is predictable. This is a good investment.' At the same time, we go to trial [prosecute] in some cases where we've alleged misrepresentations about grading and value and what we get from the industry in general is: 'Grading is subjective. Grading cannot be counted on. This is not reliable. This is not safe. This is buyer beware.'"

The FTC and the ANA have jointly produced a consumer alert pamphlet regarding rare coins as investments. Their helpful advice is contained in chapter 20.

Once you know the territory, there is potential money to be made for astute buyers and the informed collector-investors. The big question is, "What should you buy?" Helping you answer that is the sure-fire purpose of this book.

CHAPTER TWO

What Would You Recommend to Your Own Mother?

"Find out what yanks their cord. . . ."

-John Wright-

Under the category of "Only in America" you'll find the following:

1) Nearly a hundred million television viewers are enthralled by a video version of the simple pencil and paper game, "Hang the Butcher." (Let's face it, "Wheel of Fortune" is based on that kids' schooltime game, but your classmates probably didn't include Vanna White.)

2) Trusting, but unwary, investors telephone complete strangers and plead with these rare coin dealers to take their $10,000 and sell them something, anything.

I can't help you with number 1, but I'm glad you asked about number 2. Now really, do you know of anyone who has begged a stranger behind a desk at a stockbroker's office to sell him something, anything, just as long as he took his money? When it comes to stocks, bonds or real estate deals, it seems most buyers spend at least a little time investigating before they invest. They'll check out a specific stock, or a mutual fund, or at least find out something about the brokerage company handling the transaction. But when it's rare coins, almost anything goes—and usually the first thing to go is the investor's money. There are many horror stories about unsolicited telephone calls from "dealers" (boiler room operators) promising spectacular profits from coins if only the recipient of the call would buy, and buy now. The calls do not have to be unsolicited, there are plenty of horror stories about customers who thought they knew the dealership, but did not know coins. (As mentioned in chapter 1, two of the best books on avoiding these kinds of problems and preventing you from starring in your own version of a Stephen King horror story are *The Coin Collector's Survival Manual* and *The Investors Guide to Coin Trading*, both by Scott A. Travers.)

When confronted by an unusual coin, the two most frequently asked questions by non-collectors are: "What is it?" which usually is quickly followed by, "How much is it worth?" The most frequently asked question by a new collector often is, "What should I buy?" Even experienced collectors confront that same challenge. It can be a delightful dilemma. It can also lead to an exhaustive self-examination.

Collecting and investing fads come and go. In the early 1960s, many coin "collectors" purchased items by the rolls. Not just one 1950 nickel struck at the Denver Mint, but a roll of 40 pieces. Don't just purchase a single, uncirculated penny, they thought, buy a roll of 50 or even a bag of 5,000 cents. The roll-mania bubble finally burst in 1964. Some buyers still holding their purchases since then may have done quite well. If you had bought a superb quality roll of 1958 Franklin half dollars for $55, and each coin was truly an excellent (MS-65) specimen, you'd have a roll with *each* of the 20 coins worth about $50 to $70 apiece. But those 1950-D nickels, selling at one time for about $1,000 per roll, today are valued at only $250 for the entire roll of 40 coins—a little more than six bucks each.

Many dealers frequently quote the annual Salomon Brothers survey of tangible assets indicating that rare coins are an excellent investment. Yet, for every survey showing coins have appreciated 15 or 20 percent or more per year, you can find individual coins that have increased 40 or 50 percent. You also may find many that have dropped in value by 15 or 50 percent. Still, there are some coins that seem to slowly but surely increase in value over the years. Coins that have generated enough interest, intrigue and infatuation can withstand the fads and fantasies of the marketplace over the years. There are other coins that seem to be exceptionally good values now, either because they have been overlooked in the stampede to buy only trendy, "hot" items, or there just is a relatively small available supply and a potential for a larger, future demand.

Dealer Elliot S. Goldman of Allstate Coin Co., Tucson, Arizona, believes "common" coins (and so-called "generic" coins, common pieces that are slabbed) will not prevail in the long run because they are, by definition, common.

"Anything that is common can be obtained at any time in virtually unlimited quantities. Coins such as common date Morgan dollars are being graded by the major [grading] services at the rate of thousands per month and are declining in value, while scarce and rare dates within the series are excellent investments," he wrote in a guest viewpoint column in *Numismatic News.* "Coin values, just as in any other market, are based on supply and demand. Scarcity will always prevail, and the greatest value of coins in the future will be in those that are seldom available today."

This is exactly what happened to the numismatic marketplace at the start of the 1990s, an increasing demand by collectors for genuinely scarce coins. Not just what one dealer claims is scarce, but coins that really are difficult to locate, sometimes in any grade; the key and semi-key dates and mintmarks of each coinage series.

The American Numismatic Association, a nonprofit, educational organization with more than 30,000 members, provides this recommendation in its introductory booklet, *Coin Collecting—a fascinating hobby for young and old*: "Coin collecting is what you make it. Depending on your budget and area of interest—be it contemporary U.S. issues, world numismatics, medals or tokens—coin collecting can be a challenging yet affordable pastime."

The question is still frequently asked, "What should I buy?" To find the answer(s) for this book, more than 200 prominent rare coin collectors, investors, and dealers were asked what purchases they would recommend to their own mothers. The survey asked them to respond to the question: "If my closest relatives or friends wanted to get into numismatics I'd recommend they purchase the following item(s) because of their numismatic and historical importance, beauty, and potential for increasing in value." The recommendations are contained in this book, and the answers may surprise beginners as well as advanced collectors or investors.

Some respondents requested anonymity, virtually all of them private collectors who apparently fear the possibility of theft if there is publicity about their collections. Most respondents were pleased to include their names along with their recommendations.

Survey participants were invited to list up to ten recommendations. Some provided ten suggestions, some offered less. A few participants jokingly swore they would never recommend rare coins to their mothers, only certificates of deposit or other financial instruments with guaranteed rates of return and safety. A couple of dealers did not joke when they made similar comments. One respondent indicated: "If my closest friends or relatives wanted to get into numismatics I'd recommend a straightjacket for they would certainly be nuts." (That sure instills confidence in that dealer's abilities to guide his clients.) Several dealers declined to make specific copper, silver or gold coin recommendations, but did offer solid gold suggestions.

Texas dealer Jeffrey S. Zarit, who specializes in coins of

the world, declared: "Quality! Quality! Quality! It doesn't matter what. The old axiom is never more true than it is today, 'Good coins are not cheap and cheap coins are not good!' Buy the best [quality] you can afford."

American Numismatic Association vice president and *Los Angeles Times* syndicated coin columnist Edward C. Rochette suggests putting together a collection of items that have "special interest [to you] without regard to potential value." He recommends a "topical" collection, perhaps commemoratives or coins that are related by topic(s), such as coins depicting Presidents, birds, or other subject matter. Stamp collectors have been happily assembling collections by topic (topicals) for decades.

Dealer David C. Welsh of Dave's DCW Collection, Ramona, California, agrees with Rochette about the enjoyment factor. "It is important to enjoy what you are doing. Learn to grade coins to your satisfaction, slabbed or raw, and don't expect to make a profit for at least five to ten years."

David Lisot, president of Media Resource Corporation, Los Angeles, who for several years presented regular rare coin market reports on the Financial News Network (FNN) also emphasizes "Buy what you like! Compare price and know your dealer!" Lisot recommends learning "the story behind what you buy and share the story with others." What a wonderful way to spread numismatic knowledge!

A few weeks before he died, prominent California collector Nathan Bromberg pointed out "the coin collector has a hobby in which the entire family can participate. It is a lifetime hobby in which generation after generation can become involved. Thanks to the numismatist, history can be traced and preserved forever." (Mr. Bromberg was seventy-one, and a member of nineteen coin clubs. At the time of his death in March 1990 he was president of the Downey, California Coin Club and was in the process of establishing a fund to promote coin collecting among school children. He will be missed.)

John D. Wright of Michigan, an active member of the Early American Coppers club, sums up his advice in three words: Look, talk, choose. "Look at a lot of coins of all sorts—U.S. and foreign, current, Medieval, and ancient. Talk to the owners about them. Find out what yanks their cord about their specialty. With enough exposure [to all these different coins and their owners] you will fall in love with one or more aspects of this hobby. With a wide enough sampling you will be prepared to choose instead of just pursuing the one item somebody else showed you."

"As with any other field, knowledge is king," stated California survey participant Cynthia Lee Mohon.

This book is not a comprehensive listing of every coin you might consider purchasing to start a collection or add to one. Nor is this intended to be anywhere near the last word on the specific coins mentioned in the upcoming chapters. The book is intended to give you a feel for what's available, and once the numismatic bug has bitten, you are invited, encouraged, and, I hope, inspired to seek out the many other wonderful, detailed coin and currency books available. Chapter 23 contains recommendations on books, hobby magazines and newspapers, and specialized newsletters that will be invaluable resources for the beginner, the intermediate, and the advanced collector-investor. One of the frequently repeated adages in collecting is to "buy the book before [buying] the coin."

Another popular saying is, "There is no Santa Claus in numismatics," similar to warning someone there are no free lunches. Speaking of lunch, now that your rare coin buying appetite has been whetted, let's look at the best rare coins to own according to the survey.

Obverse

Reverse

A superb example of the first United States commemorative coins, an 1892 Columbian Exposition half dollar. *(Photos by James A. Simek)*

CHAPTER THREE

United States Silver Commemorative Coins

"There's a sucker born every minute."

-P.T. Barnum-

A s the host of the TV game show "Family Fued" shouts: "Survey says! The number one answer is. . . ." In this case, the survey indicates the most frequently recommended coin or coinage series was United States silver commemoratives. Surprising? In retrospect, not at all.

U.S. commemorative coins combine history, beauty (although a few examples belong in the numismatic doghouse), and a potential for increasing in value. Some are available in such abundant quantities they can be mass marketed, at least in less than gem quality condition; other commemorative issues are relatively scarce in any grade, and downright rarities in splendid condition. "Commems" have experienced more ups and downs than elevators at New York's World Trade Center. Market manipulators occasionally have tried to run up the prices, and at times commems fall out of favor of the "in" crowd, but over the decades they've developed a solid following. As collectors become more educated about their hobby they discover commems can be gems.

First issued in 1892 as a fund-raising effort to help pay for the Columbian Exposition in Chicago, the U.S. commemorative series salutes people, places, and events of importance to America, and includes gold, silver, and copper-nickel clad coins with face value denominations from 25 cents to $50. The series itself is filled with its own fascinating history about various organizations and individuals maneuvering to obtain Congressional authorization for commemorative coins and the rights to distribute them. Sometimes the history was made years after the coins were issued, such as in the 1930s when a Bronx dentist did more than fill cavities. He filled a niche in the numismatic marketplace by punching a five-pointed star on the obverse of several hundred of the 1922 President Ulysses Grant Memorial coins. Most of the originally struck coins did not have a star, but 5,000 were officially produced with them and those were worth about twenty times the value of the "plain" coins when the enterprising dentist went to work around 1935. However, his handiwork today is considered a fake.

Dealer Roger Bryan of Gainesville, Florida, thinks the genuine Grant/star coins in MS-64 condition are an excellent value. Of those 5,000 genuine pieces struck in 1922, somewhat less than 4,250 survive. The agency originally distributing them, the Grant Centenary Commission, melted 750 unsold pieces in 1923. It's interesting to note that a president with one of the worst administrations in United States presidential history now is depicted on a coin recommended as one of the best buys in United States numismatics.

With the exception of the Great Depression years and World War Two, U.S. commemoratives were issued by the Mint every year from 1922 through 1954. In 1936 alone more than a dozen different commems were struck. Dallas dealer Steve Ivy of Heritage Rare Coin Galleries described the "furious flurry" of production between 1934 and 1938 as fueling speculation in commemoratives that rivaled the speculative financial bubble over Holland tulip bulbs centuries earlier. Financial abuses connected to the efforts to construct a Booker T. Washington Birthplace Memorial with sales of the 1951 through 1954 Booker T. Washington-George Washington Carver series of commems prompted congressional and treasury leaders in Washington, D.C., to halt the entire commemorative coinage program for nearly thirty years. Requests to produce commemoratives were utterly rejected in the mid-1950s through the 1970s, except for the dual dated 1776–1976 Bicentennial design coins issued for circulation and specially made collector sets. Mint Director Donna Pope wisely recommended a second look, and commems resumed in 1982 with 90 percent silver half dollars marking the 250th anniversary of the birth of President Washington.

Sales of the 1984 U.S. Olympic and 1986 Statue of Liberty commemoratives helped raise tens of millions of dollars for both the Los Angeles Olympic games and renovation of the Statue of Liberty. Some commems were not as quickly accepted by the public, even for worthwhile fund-raising projects. The commemorative half and quarter dollars struck for the 1892-93 Columbian Exposition in Chicago each originally were sold to the public for one dollar. Most people thought they were getting better value by purchasing a Christopher Columbus 50 cent piece for a buck, so they ignored the 25 cent pieces that also were priced at a dollar each. Of the 40,000 Queen Isabella Columbian Exposition quarters struck, 15,809 went unsold and later were melted.

It is easy to understand why explorer Columbus and Spain's Queen Isabella are depicted on coins commemorating the 400th anniversary of Columbus' voyage, but why is circus baron P.T. Barnum on the 1936 Bridgeport, Connecticut, commemorative half dollar? According to Walter Breen and Anthony Swiatek in their important reference book, *Silver & Gold Commemorative Coins, 1892 to 1954*, Barnum is credited with sparking economic development of Bridgeport in the nineteenth century. Certainly, the 1936 Bridgeport commem is not the only example of a huckster involved in rare coins, but it is one of the few times the huckster actually is depicted on the coin.

Commemorative coins date back to ancient Greece and Rome where coins frequently were struck to honor various heroes and events. Early coins often were used to inform the citizens about changes in government; you knew who was in power by seeing his portrait on the coins. This was sort of like the "golden rule;" whoever was issuing the gold coins was making the rules.

Most of the commemoratives issued by the United States have real historical significance, many have beautiful designs, and all have interesting stories to tell. Commemorative coins were the most frequently recommended items among those responding to the survey with more than a third of the respondents recommending commems; silver issues in high grade being the most frequently mentioned. South Laguna, California, dealer Mike Kliman believes anyone starting in numismatics should have "at least one of the commemorative halves" in uncirculated condition.

In most cases, U.S. commems are "N.C.L.T.," noncirculating legal tender. These are coins officially struck by a government, carrying a face value denomination, but never intended for actual use as pocket change. Some collectors completely shun any other forms of NCLT, and there are plenty of examples of third-world countries issuing coins (and postage stamps) that are virtually never used in the countries from where they originate, only produced for sale to collectors elsewhere. While U.S. commemorative coins usually have not circulated (although some have), they have established themselves as an historic and important coinage series and, therefore, do not carry the stigma that usually accompanies other NCLT issues.

Although the United States resumed striking of commemorative coins in 1982 to mark the 250th anniversary of the birth of President Washington, survey respondents generally recommended purchasing pre-1955 commemorative coins. These earlier items were struck in much smaller quantities than most of the modern issues.

A few survey respondents, such as collector Charles Colver of California, recommended commemorative coins in About Uncirculated or better condition ("*NOT* in slabs," he added), but many others, including collector and former ANA Board of Governors member Bill Fivaz of Georgia, highly recommended selected commems in MS-63 or 64 grade. "Choice uncirculated or better," advised Silver Spring, Maryland, dealer Julian Leidman. In these grades, the coins should still have attractive "eye appeal," yet they usually will not have astronomical price tags.

Former Professional Numismatists Guild President Gary Sturtridge of Tonganoxie, Kansas, suggests putting together an entire set of MS-64 or 65 silver commemoratives, an adventure for a serious collector with a serious bank account with $50,000 or more of disposable income. Perhaps the beginner might want to think just a bit smaller. Oak Forest, Illinois, dealer Joseph R. O'Connor advised *MONEY* magazine readers to consider the 1947 Booker T. Washington commemorative set of coins struck at the Philadelphia, Denver, and San Francisco Mints (usually abbreviated as P-D-S) in MS-65, or the 1952 Booker T. Washington and George Washington Carver three-coin set also in MS-65. The 1947 Booker T. Washington coins might cost about $500 for all three, about $600 for the the 1952 Washington-Carver set.

Other respondents suggested higher priced items. "Commemorative halves in MS-66 and better," recommended Cincinnati dealer Mark Mendelson. "Any fully original (colorfully toned and never cleaned) commemorative in 65 or better," said dealer Steele Eunson of Monroe, Louisiana. ANA Governor Jim Halperin of Heritage Rare Coin Galleries, Dallas, likes the three-coin 1938 Texas half dollars P-D-S set in MS-65. Another former PNG president Leon Hendrickson of SilverTowne Co., Winchester, Indiana, believes any 1934 to 1938 Texas commemorative or 1936 Delaware is good to own in MS-63. (Notice, the Lone Star state's centennial commem-

Obverse   Reverse

This 1937-S Texas Centennial commemorative half dollar reminds everyone
to REMEMBER THE ALAMO. *(Photos by James A. Simek)*

oratives were struck over a five-year span. They don't do
things in a small way in that big state.)

In Janaury 1990, heated public auction bidding launched
into Earth orbit the price of a superb specimen 1923-S
Monroe Doctrine Centennial commemorative half dollar.
This particular coin was graded MS-67 by PCGS and the final
bid was $30,800—roughly four times higher than the average
price for an MS-65 specimen at the time. Not long after that
auction, retired New York dealer John Jay Ford, Jr., told
LEGACY magazine: "If . . . a guy came to me and said he
wanted to buy a Monroe Doctine half dollar for $30,000 in
Mint State-67, I'd say, 'What are you doing tomorrow after-
noon? I want to have you fitted for a straightjacket.'"

Occasionally, commems are offered for sale accompanied by their original holders. These holders can be historic
for their own sake. Collector Ralph Langham of Connecticut
recommends them. In his book, *A Comprehensive Guide to
United States Commemorative Coins*, author James S. Iacovo
noted that many of the envelopes, wooden boxes and card-
board holders that originally housed commems at the time of
their issuance have been torn, ripped, or even written upon

over the years, and coins now housed in damaged holders carry little or no additional premium. However, premium quality coins in premium quality, original holders might bring premiums of 10 to 40 percent over comparable coins without original holders. He suggested you first consider a beautiful, high grade commemorative without a holder rather than purchasing an average specimen just because it includes a holder.

Here are more of the individually recommended commemorative coins according to the survey.

Alabama "2X2" in MS-65. About 6,000 of the 1921 Alabama Centennial commems have a "2X2" on the obverse. The "X" is really the St. Andrews Cross that is part of Alabama's state emblem, and the 22 refers to Alabama being the twenty-second state in the union. There were some 59,000 other Alabama Centennial halves struck without the "2X2."

1934 Daniel Boone Bicentennial half in MS-65. 1934 was the first of five years these coins were issued to honor the 200th anniversary of the frontiersman's birth.

1892 or 1893 Columbian Exposition half MS-63 to 65. These are the first half dollar denomination commemoratives struck by the United States. In circulated grades (some were carried as souvenir "pocket pieces," others actually were spent as half dollars) they are quite common and can be obtained for $10 to $20 each, but in higher grades they are scarce and getting more costly. This coin was designed by two of the most famous and popular U.S. coinage engravers. The obverse showing a (purported) likeness of Columbus was done by Charles E. Barber, and the reverse depicting the ship, Santa Maria, was designed by George T. Morgan. At the time this book's survey was being taken, Oakbrook Terrace, Illinois dealer Larry Whitlow put together a list of "Top 15 Picks of Profits," coin series and individual dates he believed were undervalued. Among those 15 coins were Columbian Exposition half dollars in MS-63 to MS-65 grade.

1925 Lexington-Concord Sesquicentennial half in MS-65. Two of the most famous battles in American history saluted

Obverse   Reverse

When first issued in 1946, the Iowa Statehood Centennial half dollars quickly sold out; however, 1,000 of them were stored in bank vaults for release in 1996 and 2046. *(Photos by James A. Simek)*

on one coin. This issue has a high mintage, 162,013, but is difficult to find in high grade.

The 1934 Maryland Tercentenary in MS-65. A rather scarce issue with only about 25,000 pieces struck, the coin depicts Lord Baltimore, Cecil Calvert.

ANA vice president Ed Rochette believes early gold U.S. commemorative issues are an excellent area to consider. Dealer Gary Adkins of Burnsville, Minnesota, likes gold and silver commemoratives in MS-63 or 64 grades.

In 1996, watch for possible sudden interest in the 1946 Iowa Centennial half dollars. Five hundred carefully selected, high quality specimens stored in bank vaults since 1948 will be sold by the state of Iowa in 1996. Another 500 will be released for sale in the year 2046.

In June 1990, well-known commemorative coin specialists Don and Helen Carmody of Huntington Beach, California, accompanied the Iowa State Treasurer Michael F. Fitzgerald and other invited dignitaries in examining a portion of the hoard. Looking at the 500 Iowa statehood commemoratives to be released in 1996, the Carmodys described them as mostly MS-65 or better, and the rest generally were at least

MS-63. These coins sold for about $3 each back in the late 1940s. At the time the 1990 inspection was made, MS-65 Iowa coins were selling for around $350 to $400. Perhaps the 1996 release of so many high quality specimens will trigger demand for Iowa Centennial pieces, just as the Redfield Hoard and G.S.A. sales helped promote interest in Morgan silver dollars (see chapter 4).

The annual editions of *A Guide Book Of United States Coins* (known in the hobby as "the Red Book" because of its cover's distinctive color) contains an excellent, basic reference section on commemoratives. Scan the pages, look at the photographs, read the capsule commentaries about the historical significance of the coins. Maybe you'll find one that appeals to you. If so, buy it because you like it, not because silver commemoratives happen to be the most frequently recommended coins in this survey. Anyone who seeks only financial gain from numismatics—and ignores inherent hobby pleasures—should only purchase the Bridgeport commem, study it closely and remember it was P.T. Barnum who cynically stated, "There's a sucker born every minute."

To avoid falling into that category, consider joining the Society for U.S. Commemorative Coins, 912 Bob Wallace Avenue, Huntsville, Alabama 35801. Dues are $15 per year and include subscriptions to *The Commemorative Trail*, the society's informative, quarterly newsletter.

Obverse

Reverse

A magnificent example of one of America's most popular and historic coins, the Morgan silver dollar. *(Photos by James A. Simek)*

CHAPTER FOUR

Morgan Dollars

"We thought silver dollars offered the

greatest investment potential for the

1970s and 1980s."

-Les Fox-

Remember those silver dollars Grandma delightfully provided for your birthdays? Remember how you probably played with those big coins, perhaps tossing them into a shoebox or a desk drawer already crammed with your assorted marbles, rocks, bottle caps, and baseball cards? Don't you wish you had safely protected and saved all those silver dollars? Don't you wish you also had saved all those baseball cards?

The United States has been producing silver dollars of various designs since 1794. Those struck between 1878 and 1921 are highly recommended by the collectors and dealers who participated in the survey.

Silver dollars hold a fascination for collectors and non-collectors. They're big, they're often still found mint-fresh shiny, and they look and feel like they're worth lots of money. Silver dollars of the 1800s evoke an image of the Old West. They're even nick-named "cartwheels," a name that symbolizes a pioneer image. They also can symbolize some of the biggest rare coin deceptions of the twentieth century.

How many newspaper and magazine advertisements have you seen proclaiming "limited availability of genuine, hundred-year-old silver dollars"? Often the advertisers have a corporate name with the words "Official," "United States," and/or "Mint," but the fine print indicates the company has no connection with the government we know and love in Washington, D.C. The ads usually offer circulated silver dollars at inflated prices. Over-priced and over-graded spec-imens are not the coins recommended by the survey respon-dents, no matter who offers them for sale.

In 1990, one of the largest silver dollar dealerships in the country suddenly changed its "guaranteed" buy-back poli-cies and would no longer automatically purchase the un-slabbed coins it had sold customers. Some of those custom-ers promptly took their claims against this dealer to court. One customer "invested" $598,000 over several years and had been informed by the dealer his coins were worth $750,000, but when the repurchase agreement was abruptly modified he then was told the coins now were worth $300,000. The investor was quoted in the *San Diego Union* newspaper (June 3, 1990, page 3) as lamenting, "I just realized I didn't do my homework." That homework should have included reading a *COINS* magazine interview a few years earlier in which this particular dealer actually admitted he did not collect silver dollars, only sold them to clients!

With the exception of truly rare date and mintmark coins, many silver dollars traded close to their face value for years. That's why Grandma was able to get them for you on your birthdays. She probably paid face value, one dollar, at the bank. For decades, most of the Morgan dollars, struck between 1878 and 1921 and named after engraver George T. Morgan, and the Peace dollars, struck between 1921 and 1935, seemed common. You could get as many as you wanted from the neighborhood bank even though nearly 300 million silver dollars were melted by the government after World War One. Silver dollars did not widely circulate in the United States, but some collectors did enjoy them. Back in 1913, prominent collector Howard R. Newcomb wrote an article for *The Numismatist* describing major varieties of dollars struck from 1878 to 1880.

The U.S. removed silver from its circulating coinage in 1965, and Uncle Sam began selling to the public millions of the silver dollars languishing in his storage vaults. Between 1972 and 1974 the General Services Administration (GSA) conducted a big sell-off of dollars struck at the Carson City, Nevada Mint (CC). Researchers, including Leroy C. Van Allen and A. George Mallis, closely studied these and other Morgan dollars and published the results. By 1976, Van Allen and Mallis had catalogued about a thousand different varieties, known today as VAM (Van Allen and Mallis) varieties, and outlined them in an historic book, *The Comprehensive Catalogue and Encyclopedia of U.S. Morgan and Peace Silver Dollars.* Dealers such as Les and Sue Fox, Randy Campbell, and others also wrote about silver dollars, delving into the actual rarity of many dates, mintmarks and varieties, especially in higher grades. Morgan dollars developed a huge following.

More than 100,000 copies of the Les and Sue Fox *Silver Dollar Fortune-Telling* books were sold between 1977 and 1982. "We thought silver dollars offered the greatest investment potential for the 1970s and 1980s," Les Fox explained in 1983. Arguably, that prediction was accurate, but in July 1981, Fox predicted: ". . . common date B.U. (brilliant uncirculated condition) Dollars will continue to out-perform inflation and any MS-60 Morgan or Peace Dollar will be worth at least $200 in 1992. . . ." The fortune-telling crystal ball must have been a bit murky that day; common, average uncirculated Morgan and Peace dollars today can be purchased at retail for as little as $25 or $30 each.

The 1921 Morgans struck at the Philadelphia Mint have

the highest mintage, nearly 44.7 million. The lowest mintage for the series is for the proof pieces struck in 1890, just 590 of them.

Morgan dollars became tremendously popular starting in the 1960s. They could be promoted in the marketplace because there were millions of these "rare" coins available. Many dates and mintmarks literally were available by the bag, a thousand uncirculated coins at a time. Huge supplies failed to lower or hold down prices for long. In the summer of 1983, when the U.S. coin market was still struggling to recover from the devastating market collapse of 1980, the numismatic marketplace was stunned by the price a "common" Morgan dollar brought at auction. Lot #1269 at the Auction '83 sale was an 1898-P silver dollar, a common coin, but in an uncommon condition. The catalogue described it as:

"Superb Gem Brilliant Uncirculated. An incredible coin with as deep a proof-like finish as we have ever seen. The sharply struck surfaces draped with pretty rainbow toning in the iridescent shades of gold, orange, blue and just a hint of pink . . . Should set a record price."

At the time of the auction the authoritative *Numismatic News* "Coin Market" summary listed the average retail price of MS-65 1898-P Morgan dollars at $415. The frequently quoted *COIN DEALER NEWSLETTER* indicated the bid range for proof-like MS-65 specimens was $500 to $560. Despite those value guides, this particular coin sold at Auction '83 for $2,860 (including a 10 percent buyer's fee)! Another example of how rare coin buyers get downright fanatical about top quality specimens, especially when it involves a popular coinage series. Interestingly, the consignor had purchased that $2,860 coin about twelve years earlier for only $10, a price that actually was not considered cheap at the time.

Even when a silver dollar hoard comes into the market, prices eventually have gone up because the newly available coins continued to feed the fires of demand. Case in point, the famous Redfield Hoard.

Nevada recluse LaVere Redfield accumulated 407,000 silver dollars, more than enough to play a few slot machines.

He caressed his last cartwheel in 1974. When he died, zealous I.R.S. agents, who presumably could have located hidden cash on the Titanic with just ten minutes notice, discovered Redfield's coins stashed behind a false wall in his house.

Two years later, A-Mark Precious Metals Company of California paid an astounding $7.3 million for the Redfield Hoard, a heck of a lot of numismatic money back in 1976—a time when the only encapsulated coins were those embedded in lucite paperweights. A-Mark and other dealers such as Paramount of Ohio widely promoted and sold most of these coins in the late 1970s and early 1980s.

The remaining batch of 6,000 pedigreed pieces from this historic hoard was purchased from A-Mark by Blanchard and Company of Louisiana in the fall of 1988. Unfortunately, a hobby newspaper headline announcing this important transaction read: "Firm buys Redfield remainders."

"Remainders?" I thought at the time. Perhaps the Smithsonian Institution's collection has some *remnants* for sale? Or, maybe Johns Hopkins University wants to dispose of a few, *stray* Garrett coins hidden in a drawer?

Collectors frequently wonder: "How did LaVere Redfield get so many silver dollars?" They also wonder: "What the heck kind of name is LaVere?"

His name remains a mystery, but perhaps the source of the coins was an unsolicited call from a telemarketer.

Ring. Ring.

Redfield: "Hello?"

Caller: "Mr. Redfield, good day. My name is Rob Blind and I'd like to talk to you about investing in United States rare coins."

Redfield: "Coins? What kind of coins?"

Caller: "Well, silver dollars, of course! They're the hottest items on the market right now. But my company, Rare Deals on Cartwheels, has been fortunate to acquire a limited supply of bright and shiny pieces, and we can pass along the savings to you."

Redfield: "Well, I live in Reno. I can get all the silver dollars I want at a bank or casino."

Caller: "Oh, but those are just ordinary coins. We offer clients only selected, investment quality specimens."

Redfield: "What's the difference between the two?"

Caller: "Ours come in fancy holders with official looking certificates of authenticity."

Redfield: "How much are these investment quality coins?"

Caller: "They're just $29.95 each, but if you buy ten the price is only $25.00 each."

Redfield: "Well, skip the holders and the certificates. Just send me 407,000 of 'em."

Caller: "Uh, will that be C.O.D. or by credit card?"

Back to the survey. Of those who recommended purchasing Morgan silver dollars, the respondents were almost evenly split in either suggesting virtually any coin in nice condition and those who recommended specific dates and/or mint-marks in specific grades. Wolfeboro, New Hampshire dealer Raymond N. Merena placed at the top of his list Morgan dollars graded MS-63 to MS-64 and priced between $150 and $1,000 each. Leonard Albrecht, director of ANACS, stresses quality, recommending Morgan dollars that grade MS-66 or better, while Billings, Montana dealer John Diekhans thinks someone just starting out in numismatics should collect Morgans (and other U.S. silver dollars) in grades ranging from Fine to About Uncirculated. In Extremely Fine condition, a common Morgan costs not much more than an extra large pizza with several toppings, around $15. Many of the survey recommendations for Morgan dollars were in the MS-63 to MS-65 range, with most at 63 and 64 for common specimens, and 63 or better for scarcer coins. In MS-63, a slabbed, common Morgan can be purchased for probably less than $50.

In the last few years, common date, "generic" slabbed Morgan dollars have gone on a roller coaster ride, taking buyers and sellers on a trip filled with thrills and horror, depending on when the person was a buyer or a seller. In May 1989, common date MS-65 Morgans were trading among dealers at $550. In a little over a year, during the important June 1990 Long Beach, California Numismatic, Philatelic and Baseball Card Exposition, these same coins were struggling to trade at even $150 each. MS-63 slabbed Morgans often were priced at less than $35 each. When bargain hunters began seizing the opportunity, prices for the common MS-65 Morgans rose to around $200 a few days later.

Sometimes, silver coins that have been exposed to various environments oxidize in spectacular ways. While the family silverware may turn blackish, silver dollars that have never been cleaned may acquire almost rainbow toning, shades of light yellow and orange, red and even blue and green. Coins stored in paper envelopes or in coin holders with a high sulfur content may get dazzling toning. They also can get grey and black, but the ones with the gorgeous colors get that magical "eye appeal" that prompts buyers to hand over large sums of cash. Illinois collector Pete Jorstad thinks "Morgan dollars in high mint state grade with toning for sheer beauty" are an excellent recommendation.

Morgan dollars were struck at the mints in Philadelphia (no mintmark), New Orleans (O), Carson City, Nevada (CC), Denver (D), and San Francisco (S), although not every mint struck coins every year; some had limited productions, and from 1905 through 1920 no silver dollars were struck for circulation at any of the mints. Certain date and mintmark combinations, such as 1889-CC, 1893-S and 1895 (Philadelphia), are scarce in virtually any condition. A few other combinations are common in lower grades, but exceptionally rare in uncirculated condition, such as 1884-S and 1896-O.

Dealer Robert S. Riemer of Brooklyn, New York, thinks collectors can find good value in some of these "better date dollars in MS-64 which have large spreads (price differences) between MS-64 and MS-65, such as 1890-O." The MS-64 price of that coin is about $250, but in MS-65 it commands around $4,440. Now that's a large spread. Riemer recommends the coins be certified by PCGS or NGC.

A few other respondents also suggested "better dates" certified MS-64 or better. Monroe, Louisiana, dealer Steele Eunson recommended the low mintage San Francisco dollars of 1886, 1887 and 1888 in MS-64. Only 750,000 1886-S coins were struck; 1,771,000 of the 1887-S; and just 657,000 of the 1888-S. Tom Mulvaney of Mid-American Rare Coin Auctions, Inc., of Lexington, Kentucky, agrees with the philosophy of "better date" Morgans, such as 1886-S, and also suggested 1893-CC and 1894-O in MS-63 or higher grades.

Some survey respondents believe virtually any Morgan dollar can be a winner if purchased at "the right price." Robert T. McIntire of Jacksonville, Arkansas, likes Philadelphia, Denver, and San Francisco (P-D-S) Morgan dollars from 1892 to 1895 in MS-60 or better. Q. David Bowers suggested scarce dates between 1878 to 1904 in MS-63. Collector and *Chicago Tribune* numismatic columnist Roger Boye recommends Carson City, Nevada Mint Morgan dollars in MS-60 or better grades. Boye thinks any Carson City Mint coins in these grades are excellent collectibles. This mint began coining operations in 1870 and ceased production in 1893. The old mint building now houses the Nevada State Museum.

Here are other specific Morgan dollars in specific grades recommended by survey participants: 1878-S MS-65; 1882 MS-64; 1883-O MS-65PL; 1887-O MS-64; 1889-CC MS-65 or better; 1892 MS-64; and 1899 MS-64.

The beauty and historical significance of the Morgan silver dollars continue to attract collectors well over a century after these coins made their first appearance. Some specimens possess a special kind of beauty described as proof-like.

When a coin exhibits a mirror-like reflective surface, and it is not specifically struck as a proof coin, collectors call the reflective image "proof-like," simply abbreviated as PL, such as "MS-65PL." These lustrous, avidly sought specimens often command exceptional premiums above the value of a comparably graded coin without the prooflike surfaces. Occasionally, you'll see an advertisement for "semi-proof-like" silver dollars. Do you know the difference between a proof-like and a semi-proof-like coin? Would you pay proof-like prices for a semi-proof-like? Only if you were semi-conscious. Noted silver dollar specialist Steven L. Contursi of Newport Beach, California, recommended any Morgan dollars in MS-66 with a deep mirror proof-like quality (DMPL). These are stunningly gorgeous coins, and you may have to hunt twice for a specimen; first hunting to locate one that's for sale, then searching through your bank accounts to obtain the required cash to pay for it.

To determine if a Morgan dollar is proof-like or deep mirror proof-like you'll need a piece of paper with something typed on it. It doesn't matter what's written on the paper, just as long as it is legible and was either done on a typewriter or a computer printer. With coin and typewritten paper in hand, here are the ANACS guidelines for proof-like Morgan dollars.

1) The coin will present a "mirrored" appearance in all field areas, obverse and reverse. [The field areas are those parts of the coin's surface where there is no "design element" only empty space.]

2) One-sided proof-likes will *not* receive the designation. [Both sides of the coin must meet the criteria to accurately be called proof-like.]

3) Coins with "dead spots" at any field location will *not* receive the designation. Proof-likes created by heavily repolished dies are particularly prone to this problem and should be carefully checked.

4) The proof-like designation will be applied only to those coins with a final grade of MS-60 or above.

5) Regular typewriter print must be readable (unblurred at any point of the mirror) from a minimum distance of two (2) inches.

6) If typewriter print is only marginally readable at two (2) inches, the coin will *not* receive the designation.

Here is the ANACS criteria for deep mirror proof-like Morgan dollars.

1) The coin will present a "mirrored" appearance in all field areas, obverse and reverse.

2) One-sided proof-likes will *not* receive the designation.

3) Coins with "dead spots" at any field location will *not* receive the designation. Deep mirror proof-likes created by heavily repolished dies are particularly prone to this problem and should be carefully checked.

4) The "deep mirror proof-like" designation will be applied only to those coins with a final grade of MS-60 or above.

5) Regular typewriter print must be readable (unblurred at any point of the mirror) from a minimum distance of four (4) inches.

6) If typewriter print is only marginally readable at four (4) inches, the coin will *not* receive the designation.

Morgan dollars specifically struck as proof coins are rare, with annual mintages exceeding a thousand only in three years between 1878 and 1904. Perhaps not surprisingly, only one survey respondent suggested the purchase of Morgans graded PF-64 or PF-65. These kinds of coins are valued at perhaps $1,000 for "impaired" proofs that have been mishandled, to $6,000 and up for PF-65 specimens.

A proof coin usually represents a dazzling, sharply-struck example of the finest work of the Mint masters. They are carefully produced with specially prepared dies, and more than one strike is made in the coining press to make sure the design is exceptionally sharp compared to "business strikes," the coins quickly churned out for everyday circulation.

The planchets (the blank metal discs which become coins the instant they are struck by the coinage dies) are given extraordinary preparation and care. These planchets are struck with highly polished dies, crushing down two or three times with tons of pressure to create coins with boldly prominent designs and rim tops that sometimes resemble a thin wire. In fact, that is one of the first areas to examine when trying to determine if a coin is a proof strike, check for wire-like rims. Wire rims sound like fancy hubcaps for an expensive car, but some rare proof coins cost more than a car, so before you pay that kind of money you'd better make sure the coin has the diagnostics of a proof, not a business strike.

In the early to mid-nineteenth century, the mint often did not use special dies to make proofs, just polished up previously used dies. Now and then they even used the coinage die of a different date and recut one or more numbers in the die's date. Between 1817 and 1859, proof coins usually were made in small batches to fill accumulated orders. The collecting of proof sets became popular in the 1840s, and there are indications some people purchased individual proof cents and other small denominations to be given to youngsters as Christmas presents. The modern era of U.S. proof coin production began in 1936. Until 1968, nearly all U.S. proof coins were struck at the Philadephia Mint. Those struck earlier at other government facilities are known as "branch mint" proofs and generally are quite rare.

Because of the emphasis on making the best possible coins, proof dies are quickly discarded compared to dies for business strikes. For example, normal dies for making one cent pieces might produce 100,000 coins, but perhaps only about 2,500 coins will be made with an obverse and reverse set of proof dies.

Depending on the procedures used, a proof coin's surfaces can be brilliant or matted in appearance, or it may have a satin finish, perhaps even a "sandblasted" look to it.

Modern proofs from the U.S. Mint have a brilliant, frosted look. The raised portion of the design appears as though it has been sitting in sub-zero weather for hours, nice and frosty. The fields of the coin, the level surfaces where there is no raised design, reflect light like a mirror. These coins certainly look different from those found in pocket change.

When a proof coin has been inappropriately cleaned (horrors!), the mirror-like surfaces may have tiny scratches called "hairlines." If those hairlines are visible without magnification, it sharply reduces the eye appeal of the coin, and sharply reduces its value. Hairlines that are visible under five power magnification can be found on many nineteenth and early twentieth century proof coins because the coins were mishandled and so many early collectors tried to lightly enhance their coins' appearance by gently cleaning them. Very lightly hairlined proofs sometimes still can be classified as "gem" condition depending on other eye appeal, grade and strike factors.

Modern proof coins can be purchased for as little as a dollar or two each. Of course, rare and desirable proof coins can cost more than the average salary of a major league first baseman. Proof coins can be purchased individually or in sets, usually a half dozen or so coins of different denominations all struck in the same year. Logically, these are called "proof sets." For about $100 you could purchase a 1959 to 1990 set of proof Lincoln cents, each with the Memorial design on the reverse first introduced in 1959 to replace the two stalks of wheat that had been the central design theme of the coins since they appeared in 1909. If your pockets are deep enough, you could try to acquire a complete set of proof Indian head design $10 gold pieces from 1908 to 1915. That easily would run into the substantial six figures depending on the overall quality of the coins. Even if you had the money it probably would take years to locate all the needed specimens.

A proof coin is a state of the art product to be admired for its superb quality workmanship as well as its overall beauty. For some collectors, a proof Morgan dollar is the epitome of that workmanship and art.

Obverse

Reverse

An example of a nineteenth century "type" coin, a Trade dollar that was originally intended to circulate in the Orient. This 1876 dollar was struck at the Carson City, Nevada Mint. (*Photos by James A. Simek*)

CHAPTER FIVE

Type Coins of the Nineteenth and Twentieth Centuries

"A collection of this kind would be

immense in educational value. . . ."

-*Q. David Bowers*-

When it comes to collecting coins, what's your type? Since 1793, when the United States Mint began production of regular-issue coins with the striking of half-cent pieces, more than 100 different types of coins have been produced for general circulation.

One of the most confusing numismatic terms for beginners is "type coins." They do not refer to specimens churned out on a typewriter, just as the also bewildering term, "key coin," has nothing to do with a keyboard. Key or semi-key coin simply means it is an important coin of a particular series either for its scarcity, popularity, or both. Sort of like saying "flour is a *key* ingredient in making bread."

A coin "type" usually is described as a specific, major design for a particular denomination. For example, the Morgan dollar is one type of United States silver dollar. There also are Trade dollars (1873 to 1885), Peace dollars (1921 to 1935), and so on. There also can be coin types based on metallic content, for example the 1943 "steel" cents (actually zinc-coated steel) struck by the U.S. when copper supplies were needed to produce World War Two ammunition.

Many collectors enjoy the challenge of trying to assemble one coin representing each major design and denomination type produced by the U.S. Mint. Collecting "by type" is an easy way to learn a great deal about numismatics and a superb way to own pieces of American history. It is fascinating to hold a Civil War era two-cent piece and realize that the great war between the North and South led to the inclusion of the words "In God We Trust" on our coinage. Those words first appeared in circulation on two-cent denomination copper coins back in 1864. A representative example of the two-cent coins struck between 1864 and 1873 can be purchased for as little as $10 to $20 for a decent, circulated piece, and between $400 to $1,000 for a nice, red uncirculated specimen. These kinds of coins are yet another example of history you can hold in your hands!

Representative examples of most other U.S. coin types also can be purchased for modest sums. Scarcer coins in higher grades cost more, of course. A complete collection of major design types of U.S. copper, nickel, silver, and gold coins will take not only a bit of time to assemble, but also a bit of money. The owner of the Los Angeles Lakers basketball team, California real estate developer Jerry Buss, originally intended to collect "one of everything in the *Red Book*, but eventually gave up his hunt due to ill health and lengthy time periods before certain items would even become available on the market. He did manage to put together a fabulous collection that included such rarities as an 1804 dollar and a 1913 Liberty Head nickel.

A colorful type set of U.S. coins does not have to cost the same as tuition to the Harvard Medical School. You can have fun on a budget while collecting coins by type, especially if you purchase denominations of a dollar or less.

Many survey respondents recommended putting together a type set of United States coins struck in the twentieth and late nineteenth centuries. One of America's most prominent numismatists, Q. David Bowers, recommends starting a collection with "a basic type set of United States coin designs." Bowers, a former president of both the American Numismatic Association and the Professional Numismatists Guild, and the author of more than two dozen books on coins, says, "If the budget is modest, then [collect] twentieth century types. If the budget is larger, then nineteenth and twentieth century types from copper through silver. If the budget is unlimited, then gold types could be included as well. A collection of this kind would be immense in educational value and would serve as a springboard to further interest [in numismatics]."

Illinois collector Richard W. DeRobertis suggests collecting type coins in "no problem" XF-AU condition. (He also suggests staying away from all "investor oriented coins MS-63 to MS-70. I would hesitate with mixed emotions to advise anyone to enter into numismatics with the thought of 'potential increase in value,'" he warned.)

The late California collector Nathan Bromberg believed that type coins in Extremely Fine or better condition provide an excellent introduction to collecting, but he also recommended putting together a lower grade (Good to Fine condition) type set of U.S. coins that "you can pass around to show non-collectors. The purpose of this is to enjoy collecting as a hobby, and to educate and introduce others to numismatics. Many interesting stories [about the coins] can be told, and a large investment is not necessary. The rewards from coin collecting are much knowledge, lifelong friends, closer family ties, plus many hours of enjoyment in the researching and sharing of my hobby. Another bonus is that this collection may increase in value monetarily to many times the original purchase price."

The Whitman Coin Products division of Western Publishing Company, Inc., of Racine, Wisconsin, produces the familiar blue folder coin holders where collectors plug coins into the appropriate punched-out holes in the folder. These are dandy for many circulated coins, but not recommended for Mint State specimens. As an excellent souvenir of the 1990 Central States Numismatic Society's fifty-first annual convention, Whitman provided free "Twentieth Century Type Coins" folders to guests at the convention's banquet in Milwaukee. While there are many additional types and varieties that could be included, there are twenty-four different coins that fill these particular holders. These basic twentieth and late nineteenth century coin types can give a beginning or intermediate collector an excellent goal, especially if the coins are sought in higher grades.

Cents:
    Indian (1859–1909)
    Lincoln (1909–1942, 1944–1958)
    Lincoln (1943 Steel)
    Lincoln Memorial (1959 to date)

Nickels:
    Liberty Head (1883–1912)
    Buffalo (1913–1938)
    Jefferson (1938 to date)

Dimes:
    Barber (1892–1916)
    Mercury (1916–1945)
    Roosevelt (1946 to date)

Quarter Dollars:
    Barber (1892–1916)
    Liberty Standing (1916–1930)
    Washington (1932–74, 1977 to date)
    Bicentennial (1976)

Half Dollars:
    Barber (1892–1916)

Liberty Walking (1916–1947)
Franklin (1948–1963)
Kennedy (1964–1974, 1977 to date)
Bicentennial (1976)

Dollars:
Morgan (1878–1904, 1921)
Peace (1921–1935)
Eisenhower (1971–1974, 1977–1978)
Bicentennial (1976)
Anthony (1979–1981)

A more detailed collection of type coins would include many additional coins. Let's look at the nickels, for example. Instead of just one Buffalo nickel, you'd include at least two kinds, a Type One from 1913 where the buffalo on the reverse is standing on a slightly raised mound, and Type Two produced in 1913 and all succeeding years without the small mound below the bison's hooves (see chapter 6). There also would be two kinds of Jefferson nickels, the "regular" kind minted almost every year from 1938 to present, and a "war nickel" produced with 35 percent silver from 1942 to 1945 and with a large, bold mintmark placed above the dome of Monticello on the reverse. You can even get more detailed in the type set by including Jefferson nickels struck with the designers initials, FS for Felix Schlag, placed just below the obverse bust of President Jefferson (1966 to present), and coins with the mintmark moved to the obverse just below the date and just to the left of Jefferson's ponytail (1968 to present).

A type collection can be quickly assembled with one visit to the neighborhood coin shop or one order with mail-order dealer, or it can become an adventure. A common, turn of the century Indian Head cent can be obtained for about as little as a dollar, or you can buy a colorful MS-65 red and brown colored uncirculated coin for perhaps $150. Then there's the succesful bidder mentioned in chapter 1 who paid $33,000 for the finest known 1907 Indian cent. A worn Barber half dollar

Obverse   Reverse

An example of one of the varieties of Seated Liberty half dollars (1839 to 1891), an 1880 specimen with no arrows on either side of the date on the obverse, and with the motto IN GOD WE TRUST above the eagle on the reverse. *(Photos by James A. Simek)*

may cost $5 or $10, an Extremely Fine condition common date might run $150, and uncirculated pieces start at maybe $350 and up.

Also receiving many recommendations were the Seated Liberty half dollars of 1839 to 1891. There are several major types in this series by Christian Gobrecht: With and without the motto "In God We Trust," with and without arrowheads at the date, with and without bursts of sunrays in the design, and with large and small lettering. There are similar interesting varieties and types in the Liberty Seated dollars of 1840 to 1873.

A type set of this era also can include gold coin denominations. Your own collecting preferences and budget should determine what you want to include. In circulated grades, some gold coins can be purchased relatively close to their actual "melt value."

If you want to turn back the numismatic calendar a bit more, a nineteenth century type set makes an eye-opening assortment! Most non-collectors are not aware that the United States produced such interesting denominations as half-cents, the two-cent coins mentioned earlier, three-cent pieces (some in nickel, some absolutely tiny coins in silver), twenty-cent coins, and nickels that were made of silver and called "half dimes." One of the smallest regular issue (as opposed to pattern or experimentally struck) U.S. coins is the silver three-cent pieces minted from 1851 to 1873. Their vital statistics: Only 14 millimeters big (current dimes are 17.9 mm) and weighing either three-fourths or eight-tenths of a gram depending on their silver and copper content. Now that's a numismatic lightweight!

Show a few of these odd denomination coins to friends and relatives and they usually are amazed. There also are quite a few major designs of large cents, quarters, half dollars, and dollar coins to consider. Some survey respondents highly recommended eighteenth century U.S. coinage, in particular 1796 quarters in any grade. This is both the first year of issue for U.S. quarter dollars and it is a one-year-only design on the reverse, a rather scrawny eagle. Only 6,146 of these coins were struck. A worn AG-3 specimen surely will cost more than $2,000, with VF-20 coins probably bringing $15,000 or more when available in the marketplace. A number of other respondents recommended later Bust design quarters from 1804 through 1807. (The "Bust" design half dimes, dimes, quarters, half dollars, and silver dollars are called that because a significant portion of Miss Liberty's bustline is quite visible despite her clothing. Sometimes, more modest collectors will refer to these coins by the *Red Book*'s designation, Draped Bust.) Later, a cap was added to Miss Liberty's head on some denominations, and these are called the Capped Bust type.

Monterey Park, California, dealer Frank Draskovic, who first suggests historical medals as a collector's item, recommends early U.S. type coins in Extremely Fine or better. David Fanning of Fountain Square Stamp and Coin in Cincinnati suggested Bust dollars 1795 to 1803 (although the "1804" dollars that actually were struck decades later are Bust type design, too) in MS-63 or better. Dean Schmidt of Lawrence, Kansas, placed Draped Bust dollars with the small eagle (1795 to 1798) and Draped Bust heraldic eagle (1798 to

Obverse   Reverse

Obverse   Reverse

Two major types of silver dollars were struck by the Mint in 1795, the Flowing Hair and the Draped Bust. *(Photos by James A. Simek)*

1804) as numbers one and two on his survey. He suggested them in MS-65 grade, certainly coins for the well-to-do that should do well in the future. The references to small eagle and heraldic eagle indicate a change in design from the same kind of scrawny bird found on the 1976 quarters to a bold, spread-winged eagle.

No matter what condition the coins, a collection of twentieth and late nineteenth century or the more expensive eighteenth century type coins is interesting to look at, and a historic set that reflects at a glance changes in the pocket change of America. Trying to assemble a complete set of specific coins by date and mintmark can be quite rewarding, quite expensive and quite time consuming; but collecting representative examples by denomination and century just might be more your type.

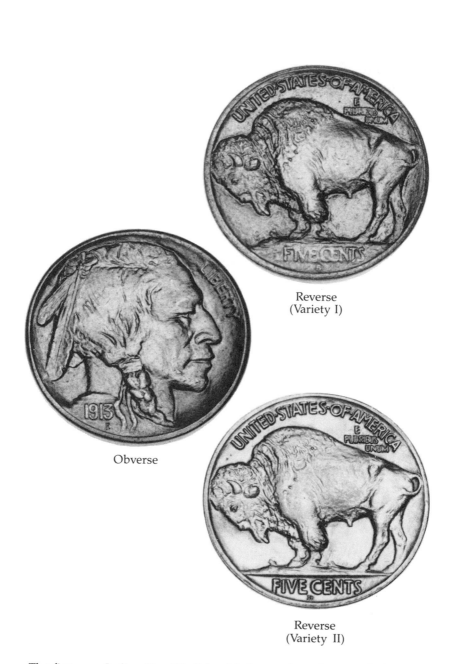

Reverse
(Variety I)

Obverse

Reverse
(Variety II)

The first year Indian Head/Buffalo nickels were issued two varieties were struck, one with the bison on slightly raised ground (Variety I), the other on flat ground (Variety II). After 1913, all of them had the flat ground design. *(Photos by James A. Simek)*

CHAPTER SIX

Buffalo Nickels

"One of the most beautiful coins

made."

- David C. Welsh -

Collectors usually refer to specific coin types by their denomination and either the *obverse* design or the designer's name; for example, the Lincoln cent and the Morgan dollar. The Buffalo nickel is an exception; the buffalo appears on the *reverse*. Struck from 1913 to 1938, these coins sometimes are described as Indian Head nickels, but not often. Then again, perhaps even the name Buffalo nickel is wrong. The animal actually is a bison.

There have been numismatic debates about the identity of the Indian on the obverse, but he's not any particular person. Sculptor James Earle Fraser reportedly used three different models for his design. However, the name of the bison is known. He's Black Diamond, a former resident of the New York Zoological Gardens, and knowing how to carefully examine Black Diamond is crucial to determining the grade of a Buffalo nickel.

Give an apparently uncirculated Buffalo nickel to an experienced collector and chances are good he first will look at the obverse only to check the date, then turning the coin over to quickly check the mintmark, he'll begin to examine the bison to determine the coin's grade. The first spot to be examined will be the hip bone and thigh just above the animal's left hind leg. Those are high points in the overall design and, therefore, the first areas of the coin's surface to experience wear. The experienced numismatist then probably will carefully look for slight wear or abrasions on the obverse at the Indian's cheekbone and his hair just above the braid. Sharpness of detail in Black Diamond's appearance can be a combination of both the actual strike of the coinage dies and any wear on the coin's surface. Because the design of the bison is so high there were problems in striking the coins. San Francisco Mint specimens are notorious for their flatness. If you can locate a sharply struck 1926-S Buffalo nickel you have located a rare coin. Sometimes you can barely see Black Diamond's horn or the end of his tail even if the coin has not encountered any other signs of wear.

There are two major types of Buffalo nickels, appropriately named Type One and Type Two. Type One, produced only in 1913, has the bison standing on slightly raised ground and the words below him, FIVE CENTS, are away from the rim of the coin. Later that year, the design was slightly modified to show Black Diamond on flatter ground, and the letters "F" and "S" in the word "FIVE CENTS" now virtually touch the rim. That's Type Two, and all Buffalo nickels produced after 1913 use this design.

Actually, Type One and Type Two should be referred to as *Variety* One and *Variety* Two because Buffalo nickels themselves represent the coinage *type*. But most collectors still call them Type One and Type Two, and really, can you expect anything else since things already are mixed up by referring to the entire coin by its *reverse* design, rather than what's on the front?

Four prominent mint errors are found in this coinage series. In 1916, there is a doubled die obverse where two distinct dates can be seen close together. There is a bold overdate in 1918 where an 8 was punched over the number 7 so the date reads 1918/7 on some Denver Mint coins. Another interesting blunder occurred in 1937, the accidental creation of a three-legged buffalo. On the three-legged variety, a portion of the buffalo's right front leg is missing because of a mistake at the mint, too much polishing of the coinage die. Around 1960 a collector discovered another fascinating mistake involving some 1938 Buffalo nickels with a D mintmark (for Denver) stamped over an existing S (for San Francisco) mintmark. Even more fascinating is that these 1938-D/S coins were in circulation for more than twenty years before someone noticed the variety! Maybe they were too busy arguing over whether it's a buffalo or a bison.

Tucson dealer Elliot S. Goldman says there are certain date and mintmark combinations that seem to be getting more difficult to locate in certain grades. In the Buffalo nickel series he cites these San Francisco Mint coins in MS-63 grade or higher: 1915, 1917, 1918, 1919, 1921, 1924, 1925, 1926, and 1927. He also likes the 1937-D "three-legged" Buffalo nickels in AU or higher grades.

Dallas dealer Jim Halperin recommends a 1913 Type One variety in high grade proof, PF-65. Dealer Mike Kliman of South Laguna, California, likes both the Type One and Type Two as proof coins. Illinois dealer Larry Whitlow, who enjoys Buffalo nickels as a personal favorite, specifically listed matte proof 1913 Type One in PF-65 or better. The special matte proof finish is not like the brilliant, mirror reflection of most other proof coins; the matte surfaces produced on some coins between 1908 and 1922 are described by the *Red Book* as a granular "sandblast" surface. High quality, matte proof coins are appreciated by connoisseur collectors.

Other survey respondents' recommendations include

purchasing both Type One and Type Two 1913 uncirculated nickels from the Philadelphia, Denver, and San Francisco Mints; any common date (for example, one person listed 1927-P) in MS-64 or MS-65; and purchasing scarce dates and mintmarks in Extremely Fine to About Uncirculated condition. Bill Fivaz of Georgia suggested the grade be "legit XF/AU," stressing the point that you must know if the coin legitimately grades in the XF or AU ballpark, or is actually something less despite what the coin holder label may proclaim.

Wymore, Nebraska, dealer Virg Marshall (affectionately known in the hobby as "The Penny Merchant") recommends Buffalo nickels in MS-60 or better grades. California dealer David C. Welsh calls Buffalo nickels "one of the most beautiful coins made [and portraying] the Indian and buffalo [brings memories of the cowboys and Indians] of the historical Old West." He likes these coins in grades ranging from AU-50 to MS-63. Illinois collector Bill Whisler describes MS-64 Buffalo nickels as "a beauty." Others suggested any "early" (teens and early 1920s) mintmarked Buffalo nickel in MS-63 or better. One survey respondent pointed out that a less expensive introduction to the series can be found in purchasing coins in grades of Very Good to Extremely Fine, although you really can't get much less expensive than common date Buffalo nickels in average Uncirculated condition. Many can be obtained for about $20 in MS-64 grade, less than $60 in MS-65. A beautiful coin at an attractive price.

In late 1977 or early 1978, before the big numismatic market rally got underway, a Chicago area dealer offered me a very lovely 1913 Type One Buffalo nickel for $50. At the time, the *Greysheet* retail price was about $35, but I paid the $50 because this was a sharply struck coin, so sharply struck it appeared it might even be a proof specimen.

The coin stayed in a bank box until August 1978, when I decided to take it to the American Numismatic Association's annual convention being held that year in Houston. During the convention I showed the coin to a dealer I respected for his knowledge about this series, and asked, "Is it a proof?"

After carefully examining the coin, he said, "It has all the characteristics of a proof, but I'm concerned about the 'E Pluribus Unum' (motto on the reverse just above the bison). It's not quite as sharply defined as you'd expect on a proof piece. Otherwise, I'd call this a proof," he concluded.

A little later, I showed the 1913 Type One Buffalo nickel to the amazing Walter Breen, the walking encyclopedia of numismatic knowledge, who had written a book on proof coinage just a year earlier, *Walter Breen's Encyclopedia of United States and Colonial Proof Coins, 1722–1977.* (This book has been revised and updated through 1989, and is a bargain at $29.95.) Breen is never far from a magnifying glass, usually wearing one on a cord hanging around his neck. He carefully took my coin, quickly glanced with his glass at both sides and almost instantly stated, "Nice proof. Did you get it here [at the convention]?"

I explained the dealer's question about the sharpness of strike on the E PLURIBUS UNUM.

Breen said authentic 1913 Type One proofs sometimes are hard to distinguish from well-struck business strikes, but that in his opinion, my coin indeed was a proof.

Later at the convention I showed the coin to another dealer who I personally admire for his knowledge of coins and the rare coin marketplace, and he immediately made an offer to purchase it on behalf of one of his clients.

"But a colleague of yours was concerned about the motto," I pointed out.

"I don't care what he said. I'm offering to buy it. Do you want to sell?" he responded. Well, he did use a few more words, some of them limited to four letters, to explain his position on this matter. But the point was clear; he thought it was a proof and would sell it to a client as such.

Checking the current *Greysheet* quotation for the coin, I sold it for $450, an amount I believed to be quite fair, especially considering I had paid only $50 for it less than a year earlier. At the time of that transaction, in the days before airline industry deregulation, the quick $400 profit virtually paid for my airline ticket and hotel room at the Houston convention.

The story could end here, but there is an ironic post-script. The next day, happily walking around the convention bourse floor with a $450 check in my name in my briefcase, I chatted briefly with another dealer whose opinions I greatly respect. I mentioned the episode with the Type One Buffalo nickel.

"How much did you get for it?," politely asked this dealer.

"$450," I proudly exclaimed.

"Is that all?" he responded. "Don't you realize how scarce Type One proof Buffalo nickels are?"

An hour or so later, I saw Walter Breen and thanked him for his assistance on the nickel, and I mentioned I was able to sell it for $450.

Genuinely surprised, Breen said, "You got *that* much!"

The lesson here seems to be Knowledge Is King. Knowledge about the coins themselves, and knowing who will pay you the most when it's time to sell.

Obverse

Reverse

Certainly one of America's most beautiful coins, the Walking Liberty half dollar designed by A. A. Weinman. This 1917-S specimen has the mint-mark on the obverse just below the motto; most others in the 1916 to 1947 series carry the mintmark on the reverse. *(Photos by James A. Simek)*

CHAPTER SEVEN

Walking Liberty Half Dollars

"A real challenge to complete."

-Anthony Swiatek-

It seems the "Walkers" are off and running again. The beautiful Walking Liberty design U.S. half dollars, minted from 1916 to 1947, usually have done quite well during numismatic boom markets. It surely is one of the most handsome of all U.S. coin designs—so nice, the government has used it twice. First, on this particular half dollar coinage series, then starting in 1986 the obverse design was used for the silver "eagle" one ounce bullion coins with a face value of one dollar. The graceful Miss Liberty with gently flowing gown walks with her right arm extended as the sun peers from the horizon. The reverse depicts a majestic eagle with wings arched over its back, a design that a few critics panned when the coin first appeared. Those criticisms have long since vanished.

Manhassett, New York, dealer Anthony Swiatek, a well-known expert on U.S. commemorative coinage, also has extensively studied the Walking Liberty half dollars. He asked me to write the foreword to his handy, little reference book, *The Walking Liberty Half Dollar.* The comments then are still appropriate now: There are Morgan dollars and there are Saint-Gaudens double eagles, so why not the Weinman half dollar?

Ask a coin collector to name a few designers of United States coinage. The response probably will be limited to the handful of designers whose names now are descriptively connected to their coins: The (George T.) Morgan dollar; the (Charles E.) Barber dime, quarter, and half dollar; the (Augustus) Saint-Gaudens $20 gold piece; and perhaps a few specialists will mention the (Christian) Gobrecht dollar of 1836 because his name was prominently—and temporarily —included as part of the obverse design.

Ask a collector to name the most *beautiful* U.S. coinage designs and the response usually will include the Saint-Gaudens double eagle. Also frequently mentioned will be the majestic Walking Liberty half dollars struck from 1916 to 1947. Why this long admired design is not referred to as the Weinman half dollar, I don't know. Perhaps the hobby's affectionate term, "Walker(s)," precludes any other description or adjective.

The designer of the Walkers, Adolph Alexander Weinman, was born in Karlsruhe, Germany, in 1870. Ten years later, he immigrated to the United States. He served as an apprentice to wood and ivory cutters, and studied under the direction of several prominent sculptors including Saint-Gaudens (that's already the fourth time he's mentioned on this page, yet his coins don't come up until chapter 9), Olin Warner, and Charles Niehaus.

To numismatists, A.A. Weinman may be best known for his popular half dollars, and for designing the so-called "Mercury" dimes that also made their public debut in 1916 (chapter 8). However, Weinman also designed stunning medals. In his superb book, *Numismatic Art in America* (Harvard University Press, 1971, Cambridge, Mass.), the curator of classical art at Boston's Museum of Fine Arts, Cornelius Vermeule, wrote: "Weinman's medals leave no room for doubt that he was an exceptionally talented sculptor."

Yet, for all his numismatic accomplishments, in 1965, the associate curator of American paintings and sculpture at New York's Metropolitan Museum of Art, Albert TenEyck Gardner, summed up Weinman's respected place in the art world by noting: ". . . he was most well known for his architectural sculpture" (*American Sculpture*, The Metropolitan Museum of Art, 1965, New York).

A.A. Weinman died in 1952 in Portchester, New York. Relatively few collectors, museums, or institutions ever can own a magnificent Weinman creation such as his statue of Abraham Lincoln at the Lincoln Monument in Frankfort, Kentucky, or even the two foot tall Lincoln "statuette" (now at the New York Metropolitan Museum of Art) he actually used to design the 1911 Kentucky masterpiece. But because of his numismatic legacy, virtually every collector easily can acquire and study specimens of his art, holding in their own hands one of America's most beautiful coinage designs: The Weinman half dollar.

The Weinman or Walking Liberty half dollars have a strong collector and investor following. At the height of the 1978 to 1980 rare coin boom market, "short sets" of uncirculated Walkers (one coin of each date and mintmark from 1941 to 1947) sold for around $4,000. A decade later, those same sets traded for around $2,300; however, superb quality, individual specimens of those years *each* can sell for that much. An average uncirculated (MS-60) 1945 Philadelphia Mint half dollar may only sell for about $25. It's a common coin. Find that same 1945-P in MS-67 condition and the price tag is probably $4,300. Interestingly, no one responding to the survey recommended that anyone start a collection with "super-grade" Walkers. Let's face it, $4,300 for the FIRST coin could scare away plenty of potential collectors. But many survey participants did recommend purchasing Walkers in grades ranging from MS-61 to 65. Some believe that slabbed MS-64 coins are attractively priced. Using 1945-P as the example, a slabbed MS-64 coin might sell for around $100, but the MS-65 version probably is priced at $350 to perhaps $400.

Former Professional Numismatists Guild President, Gary Sturtridge of Kansas, suggests a complete "short" set of 1941 to 1947 Walkers (twenty coins) as being affordable in MS-63, 64 or 65 condition. Anthony Swiatek cautions that the "intermediate" set of Walkers (1934 to 1947) "will be a real challenge to complete, and the short set will also be a challenge, especially trying to locate those San Francisco Mint coins that grade MS-65 by market and dealer standards." Trying to collect a high quality, complete set of Walking Liberty half dollars from 1916 to 1947 "will be a major undertaking," he warns.

Ohio dealer Mark Mendelson believes that pre-1930 Walking Liberty halves in MS-64 or better condition are excellent to own. Arizona dealer Elliot S. Goldman also likes certain pre-1930 Walkers. "You see mega-thousands of MS-63 to MS-66 common date Walkers being promoted, but you rarely see 1919-S, 1920-D, 1921 Philadelphia, Denver, and San Francisco, 1923-S, 1927-S, and 1928-S Walking Liberty halves in MS-63 or higher."

A few date and mintmark combinations of the Walking Liberty half series, especially the 1941-S, are notorious for being weakly struck. Even on Mint State coins, details of the design often are missing, such as Miss Liberty's fingers or even her entire hand across her waist holding the branch. Sharply struck specimens of these particular dates are quite scarce and usually command substantial, premium prices in high grades.

Obverse

Reverse

One of the key coins in the Mercury dime series (1916 to 1945) is the 1921-D. This sharply struck specimen exhibits full split bands (FSB). *(Photos by James A. Simek)*

CHAPTER EIGHT

Mercury Dimes

"The term 'full bands' is used

indiscriminately. . . ."

- Harold Kritzman -

The mythological messenger of the gods actually has absolutely nothing to do with these coins; Mercury had wings on his feet, the wings on "Mercury" dimes are on Miss Liberty's head and signify freedom of thought. This certainly is not the first instance where numismatists have not known where their heads are, or known the difference between top and bottom.

Struck from 1916 through 1945, the Mercury dime is also known as the Winged Liberty Head because of those freedom-of-thought wings sprouting from Miss Liberty's cap. These coins sometimes are referred to as "Mercs." The coin's designer, A.A. Weinman, also crafted the famous Walking Liberty half dollar which, if you can recall the lessons from the last chapter, are sometimes referred to as "Walkers." If you don't recall that lesson, either you have not yet read the exciting previous chapter, or your retention span is slightly shorter than a three minute hard-boiled egg.

Most survey respondents who recommended purchasing Mercury dimes made broad suggestions, such as recommending only a particular grade or range of grades. For example, Cynthia Lee Mohon of California likes Mercs that grade MS-64 or better. A few survey respondents suggested specific date and mintmark combinations as well as grade(s).

Harold Kritzman of Olde Towne Coin Co., Newington, Connecticut, specializes in Mercury dimes, especially those with "full bands." Full bands has nothing to do with orchestras, but being told you indeed have found a full band Merc can be music to the ears. The term refers to a portion of the design on the reverse of Mercury dimes. During the 1970s Kritzman spread the gospel about (and introduced the terms) "100 percent split bands" and "100 percent full split bands" to indicate clearly defined center horizonatal crossbands on the fasces (bundled sticks with an axe) that are the prominent design element on the dime's reverse. He emphasizes it is difficult to locate several dates of the Mercury Head dime series with these characteristics in gem quality condition.

Kritzman says the bands should not be merely fully divided, they also must have fully raised, rounded edges above the vertical sticks surrounding the axe handle. He has distributed thousands of diagrams to illustrate what to look for in these dimes. (To obtain a diagram, send a stamped, self-addressed, business-size envelope to Olde Towne Coin Co., 2600 Berlin Turnpike, Newington, Connecticut 06111.)

"Those of us knowledgeable about the Mercury Head dime series know that the 1945 [dime] was probably never made with 100 percent *full* split bands, although specimens with '100 percent split bands' have been infrequently encountered," Kritzman explains.

"We also know that the lower diagonal band on the 1916-S reverse is rarely seen struck up, even on 100 percent full split band specimens, and that the 1925-D is very rare if the 'E' at the end of 'ONE' on the reverse is fully struck up, even though coins of that date with 100 percent full split bands are not that hard to find."

Kritzman is concerned that some independent grading services are distorting the definitions of what constitutes split bands and full split bands.

"The term 'full bands' is used indiscriminately to describe both degrees of strike. Thus, one would not know from the slab services' grading whether you should expect a 1939-S described as 'MS-65, full bands' to be a scarce 100 percent split band example, or the very rare 100 percent full split bands gem coin.

"A 1942 Mercury dime in MS-65, 100 percent full split band condition is many times scarcer than a 1943-D or 1944-D in like condition. However, a 1942 in MS-65, 100 percent split bands condition is as common as the 1943-D and the 1944-D, in 100 percent full split band condition, so they are 'Bid' at the same common, or generic price.

"There are many condition rarities in the Mercury Head dime series which the knowledgeable collector can still buy at the common, full bands prices because of this lack of refinement in terminology at the major slabbing houses.

"I have found that a true full-strike, better date MS-64 was, in many cases, several times scarcer than a clean-surfaced, MS-65 with typical flat bands or soft obverse," he advised.

ANACS uses these criteria for the designation Full Split Bands on Mercury dimes:

1) The coin will exhibit all other criteria normally required for "sharply struck," with no visible weakness throughout the design on either side. [Obverse—Liberty's hair detail.]

2) All three bands on the fasces will display a complete, unbroken split with absolutely no interruptions to the horizontal lines.

3) When viewed from the side, all three bands will show some degree of "rounding" to differentiate the designation from "split bands" (split, but flat bands), a less frequently used commercial designation.

4) The Full Split Bands designation will be applied only to those coins with a final grade of MS-63 (or PF-63) or above.

Illinois dealer Joseph O'Connor recommends the 1935-D dime in MS-65 with full split bands. Kentucky dealer Tom Mulvaney thinks any Merc with full split bands in MS-63 or higher is a good candidate for a coin collection, while former American Numismatic Association Governor Bill Fivaz of Georgia listed Mercury dimes in "MS-65 (not necessarily full bands)" near the top of his survey questionnaire. John Sanders of California recommended Denver and San Francisco Mint dimes from 1917 to 1931 in grades of MS-62 through 64 with or without full bands.

Arizona dealer Elliot S. Goldman believes Mercury dimes represented the most underrated and underpriced U.S. coinage series, especially scarce and rare dates such as 1916-D in Fine or better, and the following coins in any Mint State grade with or without full bands: 1917-D, 1917-S, 1928-D, 1928-S, 1939-S, and the overdates, 1942/1, and 1942/1-D. (During the early part of World War Two, the Philadelphia and Denver mints used coinage dies dated 1941 and stamped the number "2" over the last digit in the date; hence, 1942 over 1, usually written as 1942/1.)

Chicago dealer Ned Fishkin of Carson, Pirie, Scott and Co., also likes the key date 1916-D dime in Fine to Extremely Fine grades, and recommends it be "slabbed" by one of the major grading services. Fishkin believes this coin is "underrated" and "has both a collector and dealer base to provide price support and stability."

Dealer Raymond N. Merena of New Hampshire recommends virtually all Mercury Head dimes prior to 1930 in MS-63 or 64. Ohio dealer Mark Mendelson also likes pre-1930 Mercs, but suggests buying them in MS-65 or higher grades.

Montana dealer John Diekhans thinks Mercury dimes in Very Good to Extremely Fine condition are underpriced compared to other coins that receive heavy promotion in the marketplace. Prominent Texas collector Lyman Bartee suggests Mercs in About Uncirculated or higher and also suggests proof pieces. Surprisingly, no else in the survey mentioned proof Mercury dimes. Proof coin production, generally halted in 1915, resumed in 1936 at the Philadelphia Mint. Mercury dime proof pieces are rather scarce, only struck from 1936 until 1942 when proof coin production was halted because of World War Two. According to Mint production records, a combined total of 78,648 proof dimes were struck during those years. Both the Mercury dime and the Walking Liberty half dollar are scarce "type coins" in blemish-free proof quality, and the Walkers actually have a slightly lower total proof mintage from 1936 through 1942, only 74,400 pieces.

Obverse Reverse

Obverse Reverse

The gorgeous Saint-Gaudens design United States $20 denomination gold pieces! In the first year of issue some specimens, such as the high relief variety shown here, had the date written in Roman numerals, while others were written as 1907 in Arabic numerals. There also are slight design differences on the reverse of these two varieties. *(Photos by James A. Simek)*

CHAPTER NINE

Saint-Gaudens Double Eagles

"I think our coinage is artistically of

atrocious hideousness."

- President Theodore Roosevelt -

While many numismatists believe the most beautiful silver United States coin is the Walking Liberty half dollar of 1916 to 1947, the winner in the gold coin category usually is the Saint-Gaudens $20 gold piece of 1907 to 1933, named for its designer, sculptor Augustus Saint-Gaudens. (I'll mention this again because I find it so fascinating. A handful of coins actually have become known by their designers, such as the "Saints" $20 gold pieces, the Morgan dollars, Gobrecht dollars, and the Barber dimes, quarters, and halves. Yet, you don't hear anyone refer to Standing Liberty quarters as "Mac-Neils" or Memorial design Lincoln cents as "Gasparros.")

Twenty dollar denomination gold

pieces are called double eagles, which makes a lot of sense because $10 denomination coins are referred to as eagles, which does *not* make a lot of sense because most other United States coins also have eagles on them but only the gold coins have that nickname. Five dollar denomination gold pieces are half eagles, $2.50 coins are quarter eagles. Tiny one-dollar gold coins are just called "gold dollars." Obviously, enough is enough; no one thinks "eighth of an eagle" sounds sane.

There basically are two kinds of Saint-Gaudens double eagles, those from 1907 with the date written in Roman numerals, and 1907 and later issues with the date written in Arabic numerals, 1-9-0-7. There are early specimens struck with higher relief designs, some known as Ultra High Relief. (How do you spell relief? S-A-I-N-T-S.) There are some other differences, such as wire-like rims, lettering on the edge of the coin, and slightly modified reverse design. No matter which variety or type, the Saint-Gaudens U.S. $20 gold coin certainly is one of the most gorgeous designs, and a coin whose history has a direct link to the White House.

Not all that glitters is gold. Sometimes the glitter is the publicity associated with the gold. A U.S. $20 gold piece dated 1907—with the date written in roman numerals—reportedly changed hands in 1990 for $1.5 million, setting a record. The seller is claiming this is the first legal tender U.S. coin to sell for more than a million dollars. Keep in mind this was a private transaction, not a public auction, therefore, buyers and sellers are free to proclaim whatever value they wish on this particular coin. "Prices realized" hanky-panky also is reported at some numismatic auctions, so the actual value of some rare coins changing hands that way also may be a bit suspect. Anyway, news reports of the $1.5 million double eagle's sale focused even more attention on this popular coinage series.

The Saint-Gaudens double eagles were designed by world-famous sculptor Augustus Saint-Gaudens at the request of President Teddy Roosevelt. Only about 11,000 specimens were struck of the beautiful 1907 $20 gold piece with the date written in Roman numerals. Even a somewhat worn specimen, if you can locate one for sale, probably would carry a price tag of $4,000 or more. The particular coin that reportedly traded for more than a million dollars is an Ultra High Relief specimen graded Proof-68 by Numismatic Guaranty Corporation (NGC). To achieve the sharpness of design details and the amazingly raised design surfaces, the coin had to be struck nine times in the coin press! This coin was sold in 1985 (at Auction '85) for $286,000 and its value shot up more than 400 percent in five years to $1.5 million. However, more common specimens of the lovely Saint-Gaudens gold pieces from that same era, with the date written as Arabic numerals, can be purchased for much, much less. In MS-61 or 62, common Saints trade rather close to their bullion value, often within $100 of their gold content. Jonathon M. Krasny of Beverly Hills, California, recommends PCGS-certified MS-62; dealer Jeffrey F. Bernberg of Rare Coin Company of America, Willowbrook, Illinois, listed slabbed Saints in MS-61 or 62 grade. Several survey respondents, such as John Saunders of Mission Viejo, California, and Sycamore, Illinois, dealer Bob Rozycki suggested purchasing AU-55 to MS-62 Saints at a small premium above their bullion melt value. Saunders advised a guideline of 5 to 15 percent.

Between 1876 and 1905, Augustus Saint-Gaudens designed more than four dozen medallions. His proposed design for a new one cent piece in 1907 was not accepted, but his artistry is beautifully depicted on the eagles ($10 denomination) and double eagles ($20) of 1907 to 1933. The 1933 double eagles are not legal to own. Although more than 450,000 were struck, none officially were placed in circulation because of the presidential order of April 5, 1933, regarding private ownership of gold.

Heritage Rare Coin Galleries of Dallas wrote a wonderful, brief description of a particular 1907 High Relief Saint, and that description captures the lore of the entire Saint-Gaudens $20 gold piece series. Here is a portion of that narrative.

History and art—two intertwined forces that affect
each of us. They define our culture, and the tangible
remnants we leave behind tell future generations how we
perceived ourselves and our place in the world.

'The American Century' was ushered in by a young
and energetic Theodore Roosevelt. During the Spanish-
American War 'Teddy' had become a national hero in
1898 in that 'splendid little war' that wrested several
overseas colonies from the moribund Spanish empire. He
personified Brash, Aggressive, and Innovative.

Roosevelt looked at the staid coinage designed by
Charles Barber that circulated at the turn of the century
[and felt a change was needed]. He saw an opportunity
to make it [U.S. coinage] more closely conform to the
country's new role as a world power in the twentieth
century. In a letter to Secretary of the Treasury Leslie
Mortier Shaw in December 1904 he wrote, 'I think our
coinage is artistically of atrocious hideousness.' Thus,
Roosevelt had presented a problem to which he would
soon find a solution.

In the winter of 1905, Roosevelt convinced America's
most renowned sculptor, Augustus Saint-Gaudens, to
assume an active interest in the redesigning of the
nation's coinage. Both men sought to emulate the high
relief and artistic achievement of Greek coinage struck
during the reign of Alexander the Great. Drawing from
classical Greek sources Saint-Gaudens could find no
better symbol for Liberty and the vitality of twentieth
century America than the Winged Victory (Nike) of
Samothrace (second century B.C.). He translated Nike's
striding, windswept transparency into a circular compo-
sition on the twenty-dollar gold piece that gives the coin
the dynamic effect that has so enchanted generations of
collectors. The design is now almost universally considered to be the most beautiful ever produced for a coin.

Mint personnel resented any outside artistic interfer-
ence and, as a result, development slowed almost to a
halt. Nine months after the striking of the pattern Ultra
High Reliefs, Roosevelt was impatient to see his "pet
crime" turned into actual coin form. Saint-Gaudens was
dead by that time and it was left solely to the president to

see that the sculptor's design was struck and circulated. Predictably, Chief Engraver Charles Barber resisted producing the new coins. By November 1907, production began—in high relief.

To strike high relief coins it was necessary to use the hydraulic presses the Mint usually reserved only for medal production. This was a costly and time consuming procedure and a month's work by Mint employees produced only 11,250 coins. On December 22, 1907, two coins were presented to President Roosevelt, presumably to be used as Christmas presents. Apparently these were so popular that another seventeen were sent to him on December 27. A final shipment of eight High Reliefs were charged to Mint Director Frank Leach the following day. Of the seventeen coins sent to the President on December 27, six were given out to friends, the remaining eleven were returned to the Mint. All of the delivery and return details are contained on a 3.5 by 4.375-inch card that is imprinted "The White House, Washington" in the upper right corner. The card's function was to be a receipt for the seventeen coins delivered December 27.

In 1990, Hertiage Rare Coin Galleries of Dallas acquired the finest known specimen of a regular production High Relief Saint-Gaudens design $20 gold piece. The coin was accompanied by the actual White House card and receipt for the seventeen coins delivered after Christmas 1907! The coin was submitted to PCGS for grading and was judged to be MS-68 (NGC also rendered an opinion of MS-68, but the coin was slabbed by PCGS). To date, no other High Relief double eagle has received a grade that high, although a "regular" strike 1910-S did merit MS-68. As Heritage officials pointed out, the previous owners of this particular coin understood its historical significance. "Over the decades, the owners obviously desired to preserve the coin, much as others would care for a Monet [painting], Chippendale furniture or a Bugatti [automobile]. High Relief double eagles are among the most difficult of all coins to maintain in top condition. The softness of the gold and the high relief of the design

Evidence of President Teddy Roosevelt's direct involvement in the Saint-Gaudens double eagle is this December 27, 1907, White House receipt for seventeen of the newly-struck coins. *(Photo courtesy of Heritage Rare Coin Galleries)*

make them virtually impossible to preserve in top condition over long periods of time."

This particular specimen was valued at $750,000 and Heritage proudly described it as "The Ultimate American Coin."

While very few collectors have the ability to pay three-quarters of a million dollars for such a superb coin, remember that all Saint-Gaudens double eagles are desirable as individual works of art, as tangible historical artifacts that trace their origins (and in the case of the specific coin above, their pedigree) to President Theodore Roosevelt, and they represent the beginning of a truly modern coinage.

Something to ponder about double eagles and all other U.S. gold coins. According to Coin World's *Comprehensive Catalog & Encyclopedia of United States Coins*, between 1793 and 1933, the United States struck more than $4.25 billion worth of gold. That's billion, with a "b." However, most of it has been melted. Less than $300 million worth of gold coins remain!

Obverse

Reverse

Alexander the Great spread an empire—and coinage—throughout the ancient world. This is a silver tetradrachm. *(Photos by James A. Simek)*

CHAPTER TEN

Ancient Greek and Roman Coins

". . . rulers whose names have become

household words."

- Dr. Arnold R. Saslow -

By court order, the acclaimed collection of ancient Greek and Roman coins owned by (in)famous oil and silver market barons Nelson Bunker Hunt and his brother William Herbert Hunt was sold at auction starting in June 1990. The first 899 auction lots brought a total of $12,797,000 (including a 10 percent buyer's fee). That's an average of more than $14,000 per coin! The highest bid was $572,000 for a decadrachm of Agrigentum, one of only eight known specimens of these impressive, large silver coins and only the second time in ninety years that one of those specimens was offered in a public sale. Another decadrachm, also large, also impressive, and hand-struck in Athens more than two thousand years ago, sold for $528,000 in the sale conducted by Sotheby's.

The wealth of ancient Greece again changed hands, bringing attention to the beauty and value of many ancient coins. Yet, despite those huge prices paid for the Hunt brothers collection, anyone can obtain a genuine, 2,000-year-old ancient Roman coin for as little as $10. That's not a misprint, $10; maybe even a little less. No, the coin will not be Mint State. Yes, you might have trouble specifically identifying it by exact type or die variety because of its worn or corroded condition. But where else in the collecting world can you obtain an authentic ancient artifact for so little money? Decent quality ancient coins, even some silver pieces, easily can be obtained for $100 to $200, certainly for less than $300 each. Even some gold coins of this era can be obtained for a few hundred dollars each, although if you are seeking better quality specimens or exceedingly rare coinage types, such as those from the Hunt brothers, you'll have to add one or more zeros to the figures cited above. In collecting ancient coins, there is something for everyone's budget.

Ancient coins also enjoy widespread appeal, not just in Europe and the United States. In 1981 I attended my first Numismatic Symposium conference in Sydney, Australia, and realized firsthand the global popularity of ancients. The conference included an auction conducted by one of Australia's largest dealers, M.R. "Bob" Roberts. Between 400 and 500 people filled a downtown Sydney hotel ballroom for that sale, and when ancient Greek and Roman coins were offered there were scores of bidders for each auction lot. Here I was, literally on the other side of the world, when I suddenly realized the virtually universal appeal of these classic coins for knowledgeable collectors.

There generally are six broad areas of "ancient" coinage: the famous Greek city-states such as Athens and several hundred other towns, the Roman Republic, the Roman Empire (hail, Caesar!), the Byzantines, the barbarians, and the ancient Orient. This brief chapter looks at recommendations involving ancient Greek coinage from around 600 B.C. until around 200 B.C. (with the period sometimes described as "the finest art" from around 450 to 350 B.C.), and Roman coinage from the Roman Republic of 200 B.C. through the Imperial period until the end of the Roman Empire around 600 A.D.

Around the seventh century B.C. someone in Asia Minor began making coinage in the form of rather crude, little chunks of a gold and silver alloy, electrum, that were stamped on one side with rectangular marks. Eventually, the coinage went from crude to grand. The art of ancient Greece and Rome is reflected in the coinage with magnificent designs of mythological figures, symbolic animals, flora and fauna, and eventually the political and military leaders of the day. Sometimes their wives and other family members were honored on the coins. Alexander the Great not only spread Greek culture, he spread Greek coinage, too. Examples of this coinage with Alexander's portrait, such as 2,200-year-old silver tetradrachms in Very Fine condition, can be purchased for as little as $300 to $400 each.

The decline of these ancient civilizations also is reflected as the artistry goes from brilliant, high style to crude carelessness, and the coinage becomes debased with precious metal content either reduced or eliminated.

Some collectors of ancient Roman coinage try to assemble a collection by the portrait of the emperor or other historical figures depicted on the coins, such as Marc Antony and Brutus. In a few cases, coins of particular emperors are rather scarce because the rulers didn't rule very long. Roman Emperor Pertinax lasted only eighty-six days on the throne in the year 193 A.D. before being murdered. Wisconsin collector William Pettit reminds us "there are some ancient rulers about whom we have no other record except that their portraits and names appear on coins!"

Collectors with larger checking accounts may strive to collect one of each of the well-documented "12 Caesars" of Rome: Julius Caesar, Augustus, Tiberius, Caligula, Claudius, Nero, Galba, Otho, Vitellius, Vespasian, Titus, and Domitian. It can be an exciting adventure to obtain all twelve on silver coins, and for around $100,000 a collector can purchase the 12

Caesars in gold, a classic collection reflecting the glory as well as the depravity of ancient Rome.

"An area of the ancient world which has long fascinated both the historian and the collector of ancient coins is the period known as 'The Time of the 12 Caesars,'" explains Dr. Arnold R. Saslow, director of Rare Coins & Classical Arts Ltd., South Orange, New Jersey, and Palm Desert, California. "Starting with Julius Caesar, who was assassinated on the famed Ides of March in 44 B.C., we go through a group of familial-related rulers whose names have become household words. It is a period of great victories, dark intrigues, suicides, assassinations, poisonings, and aberrant spousal relationships that seems to hold a dark fascination for us today. Man has always been attracted to shiny metals, and, of course, it is natural for there to be great interest in gold coins of these famous rulers."

One of these gold coin sets made international headlines in 1990. These particular coins were a previously unknown gift to President Chester A. Arthur in the 1880s, and they made their public debut under armed guard at the annual Chicago International Coin Fair in March 1990. The gift to President Arthur was a unique presentation set of the gold aureus coins of the 12 Caesars of Rome. (One gold aureus was equal to twenty-five silver denarii, and one silver denarius was equal to sixteen bronze asses. No, not metal statues of a donkey, the bronze "as" was a coin denomination during the Roman Imperial period. There are other major denominations, too, such as the bronze sestertius that was equal to four bronze asses. The coinage denominations can be nearly as complicated as the political histories of ancient Greece and Rome. In fact, they record those histories!)

The President Arthur 12 gold Caesars rare coins are housed in purple, crushed velvet inside a specially-made, black leather case inscribed with gold lettering: "Presented by Wm. Waldorf Astor, Minister of Italy, to Chester A. Arthur, President of the United States."

President Arthur, who took office following the assassination of President James Garfield, served from 1881 to 1885.

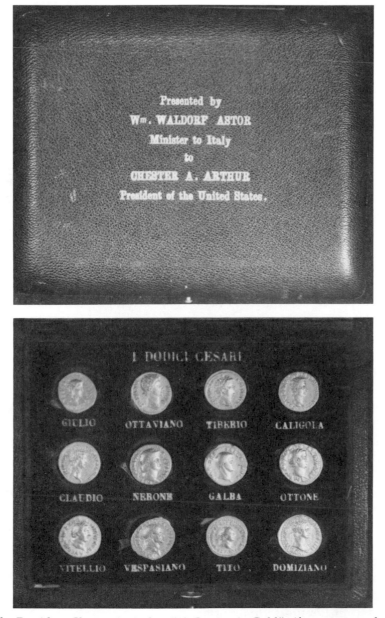

The President Chester A. Arthur "12 Caesars in Gold" gift set presented to him by his ambassador to Italy, William Waldorf Astor. *(Photos courtesy Superior Stamp & Coin Co.)*

Ambassador Astor, for whom the famous Waldorf-Astoria Hotel in New York is named, was appointed Minister to Italy by President Arthur.

"This set is without any precedent in the history of the collecting of ancient coins," said Dr. Saslow, one of the two current owners of the presentation set. "It is a unique piece of numismatic Americana."

George Beach, director of Numiscellaneous, Owosso, Michigan, discovered the set in the possession of a Florida family in 1989. "This set is the most extraordinary thing to come along in my career as a professional rare coin dealer," he explained. It is the most important item I've purchased in more than twenty years in the business. Nothing has approached the thrill and the excitement of this historic set of gold coins."

The historic set now is jointly owned by Dr. Saslow and Ira M. Goldberg, a partner in Superior Stamp & Coin Co., Inc., Beverly Hills, California. The current owners have placed its value at $250,000, although there is some controversy over the authenticity of one of the twelve coins.

Publications in the United States, Canada, Europe, and Australia gave prominent coverage to the discovery of this set. The monthly *Australian Coin Review* even published a full color photograph of the set on its front cover. The set again attracted news media attention when it was placed on display in Seattle at the American Numismatic Association convention in August 1990.

Here certainly is an example of both the importance of select, ancient Roman coins—then and now—and, an example of how these particular coins have a direct link to United States history; a prestigious gift to a President more than a century ago. No other ancient coins may have such a connection to United States history, but all of them do represent a direct link to the rise and fall of earlier civilizations, the very beginnings of democracy, "international" conquest and trade, and exalted ideals of art.

A crucial eye-appeal factor when looking at ancient coins is style, especially "fine style." Chicago dealer Harlan J.

Berk, who writes the award-winning "What's Old" column for *World Coin News*, provides the best answer I've encountered to the important question, what is fine style? Here is Berk's explanation:

"Fine artistic style for coins is simply a matter of being able to judge drawing and sculpture, nothing more or less. If a coin is well drawn, it is of good style; if, though, it is sculpted as well, then it can be of great style. The drawing or lines of a portrait or figure give it boundaries and shape, but relief or sculpture give it life. Great style, then, is well drawn and of such relief that is seems literally alive.

"There is an easy test of fine style. Ask yourself this question: If what I am looking at now—a portrait of Philip II or a horse of Larissa—were brought to life, then could it survive? The answer is, no, if Philip has no eye or mouth. The answer is, no, if a horse has only three hooves or a back leg that is so thick it wouldn't move the horse properly. If, though, in life, all things function well, then it probably is fine style. Though difficult to explain, sensitivity and delicacy are important elements of best style at the highest levels of numismatic art.

"In Greek times the best die cutters were too expensive for most cities to employ on a permanent basis. When a city had great wealth it would employ an artist to cut dies for it. It is my theory that after this individual left, local artists would copy the master's work from coins struck with his dies. They would make the next set of dies using their own coins as models, thus getting further away from the original.

"A Roman coin of fine style usually requires a life-like portrait. Brutal realism is the mark of the best style of Roman coins which can most often be seen easily and consistently in coins of Vespasian and Nero. Caligula, I feel, is the individual of whom some of the best portraits were ever produced in the Roman world. They are finely modeled, but the element that makes them great is the eyes. The mindless, cruel, even wild expression telegraphs an urgent message describing the emperor's mental state, not only to his people, but to us nearly two millenia later.

"Occasionally, a portrait of an emperor is too Hellenized and refined, as in the case of Julius Caesar. In some dies he looses his wrinkled neck, large Adam's apple, and gaunt face for a refined, fleshed-out, god-like Hellenistic portrait. This is good Hellenistic art, but bad Roman portraiture.

"There is a way to test your eye on some Roman issues to know if the portrait on the obverse is of good style or not. Sometimes, if the obverse portrait is exceptional and if the emperor is portrayed as a standing figure on the reverse, the face of the standing emperor can be recognized clearly as the emperor's portrait even though that portrait may be only two millimeters in size.

"Fine style combined with high grade (Extremely Fine or better) can translate to high values. A coin of the finest style can be struck with worn, rusty or damaged dies. If this is the case, it doesn't mean the dies were not of fine style, it just means the coin with these faults has less value. The same can be said for wear or scratches. They affect value, but are separate from art."

Here are some recommendations from the survey. Maryland dealer Julian Leidman, known as a connoisseur of United States regular issue, proof, and pattern coinage, thinks ancient coins in Extremely Fine or better condition also are among the items that can offer collectors historical importance, beauty and safety in investment. California dealer Samuel L. Lopresto, who runs the fabulously successful Long Beach coin, stamp and baseball card shows, suggests "all ancient Greek and Roman gold and silver coins in Extremely Fine or better." New York dealer and Professional Numismatists Guild President Harvey Stack also recommends ancient Greek and Roman silver coins. Colorado collector William F. Spengler put classical Greek coins at the top of his survey, then listed Roman coins next "for their historical interest and their being so inexpensive."

Wisconsin collector Paul Green points out many people enjoy the coins of the Bible. For $200 to $300 you can purchase a Fine condition silver tetradrachm from the Phoenecian city of Tyre. These are believed to be the kind of coins referred to as the "30 pieces of silver" paid to the traitor, Judas. Silver shekels of Tyre were struck starting in 126 B.C. There are many other biblical coins such as those from the reign of Pontius Pilate, and there are coins directly related to the ancient Jewish revolts, and so on.

(Paul Green also jokingly recommends the usually crude designs of Byzantine gold coins because "it shows I could have made it in art.")

Red Book editor and American Numismatic Association Governor Kenneth E. Bressett recommends a tetradrachm of Tyre and the purchase of an ancient Roman denarius in Almost Uncirculated condition. Uncirculated ancient coins are available. A few thousand years ago, neighborhood bank safe deposit boxes as we know them today just were not around, so in times of trouble many people buried their valuables. Hoards of Mint State and nearly Mint State coins, often thousands of items at a time, frequently have been unearthed.

Quarryville, Pennsylvania, dealer Kerry Keith Wetterstrom, a specialist in ancient and Medieval coinage with Classical Numismatic Auctions, Inc., recommends an Alexander the Great tetradrachm in Extremely Fine or better and a tetradrachm of Athens, also in XF condition or better. The Athenian tetradrachm is one of my favorites. Until the Peloponnesian War in 431 B.C., the city-state of Athens virtually dominated the Mediterranean. Silver tetradrachms of Athens, with the goddess Athena on the obverse and a large-eyed owl on the reverse, circulated throughout the region. Today they can be purchased for as little as $300, although a well-struck, well-centered, well-preserved specimen will cost more than $1,300.

Michigan collector John D. Wright, well-known in the hobby for his scholarship on early American copper large cents, also believes collectors should consider Roman bronze "as" or sestertius pieces in the $15 to $75 price range, Roman and Greek silver denarii in the $35 to $100 range, as well as a drachm of Alexander the Great.

Imagine holding and owning coins such as these, or one

Obverse   Reverse

An example of a silver tetradrachm of ancient Athens struck between 449 and 413 B.C. *(Photos by James A. Simek)*

bearing the contemporary likeness of someone such as Nero! You don't need a quarter of a million dollars. Bronze coins of Nero are easily obtained for a few hundred dollars, although superb quality and rare varieties in silver or gold will cost thousands, or tens of thousands of dollars. Next time you visit a coin show or leaf through a dealer's price list or auction catalogue, look at the ancient coins. Think about who and what are depicted on them and the circumstances under which these coins were struck.

Whether it's a coin for $20 or $20,000, with ancient Greek and Roman coinage you get a lot of history you can hold in your hands.

As this book was being written, no major grading service was slabbing ancient coins, and the enthusiastic cheering you may hear is from grateful collectors and dealers of ancient coinage who apparently want nothing to do with encapsualted emperors.

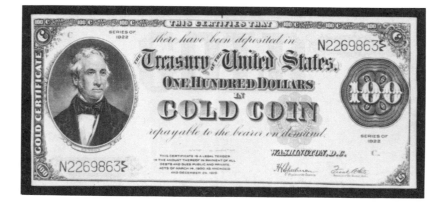

Two of the fascinating kinds of United States paper money you can collect, a National Bank Note (series 1882) issued on May 23, 1885, by the National Bank of Bangor, Maine, and a series 1922 large sized, large denomination $100 gold certificate. *(Photos by James A. Simek)*

CHAPTER ELEVEN

Currency

"This is a do-as-I-say, not a do-as-I-do

proposition."

- Charles G. Colver -

A round 1976 the Bureau of Engraving and Printing, the federal agency whose printing presses continually churn out U.S. paper money and postage stamps, was having numerous quality control problems. All kinds of mistakes were being made during the money printing process, and many of those error notes were somehow getting out to the public, and collectors.

A woman buying groceries in a Dallas area supermarket about that time was given a ten dollar bill in her change by the checkout clerk. She looked at the bill, then indignantly handed it back to the cashier demanding she be given "a real piece of money." The cashier quickly examined the note and saw it was printed

Ever see a "$30" bill? This valuable error occurred when a sheet of currency got mixed up between the printings of the front and back sides. *(Photo courtesy Harry J. Foreman)*

as a ten dollar bill on the front, but twenty dollars on the back. A "thirty dollar" bill. She placed it to the side inside the register and gave the customer another ten dollar bill, one printed correctly on both sides.

Before leaving the register at the end of that shift, the wise checkout clerk substituted one of her own ten dollar bills for the strange one the customer had angrily rejected earlier in the day. Sometime later she sold the spectacular error note for several thousand dollars.

U.S. paper money is printed several times before it is ready for distribution. First, the back side is printed, then, when the ink dries, the front; finally, the large sheet of paper with thirty-two uncut bills on it is run through a press again to print such things as the serial numbers, district numbers and seals. Somewhere between the front and back side printings, one sheet got switched from the stack of ten dollar note sheets to the twenty dollar stack. The bills eventually were cut into individual notes, bundled, and sent to the Federal Reserve Bank in Dallas.

A total of sixteen of these particular thirty dollar bills have been discovered over the years. What happened to the other sixteen that also were mistakenly printed on the sheet? It is assumed that once they learned of the embarrassing and valuable mistake federal officials were able to track them down within the banking system before they were released into general circulation, and then the unreleased notes were destroyed.

Sixteen others either were discovered by alert bank tellers before being recalled by Uncle Sam, were found in circulation by exhilarated collectors, or happily exchanged for another ten spot by a customer-pleasing, Texas supermarket checkout clerk.

While paper money was the ninth most recommended area in the survey results, there was a wide range of specific currency fields suggested by the participants. The numismatic area of syngraphics—paper money—indeed is a large one. Large sized notes measuring 7.42 inches by 3.13 inches printed before 1929, small sized notes measuring 6.14 inches by 2.61 inches produced since 1929, fractional currency with denominations of less than one dollar produced during the coin shortages of the Civil War era, National Bank Notes (explained later), and even "star" notes (also explained later) were frequently mentioned by different respondents. Prominent National Bank Note collector and Mayor of Covina, California, Charles G. Colver, listed that area fourth out of five recommendations on his survey behind commemoratives, type coins and U.S. gold. "Since I only collect U.S. paper money, this is a do-as-I-say, not a do-as-I-do proposition," he humorously explained.

The Bureau of Engraving and Printing (BEP) began its existence in 1862, a full ninety years after the Mint started making coins. Obviously, the paper money we commonly take for granted today was not always part of American history. The federal government did not produce paper money for general circulation until the Civil War when people were hoarding copper, silver and gold coins. The notes issued by the government had green-colored ink on the backs and that's when the familiar term "greenback" became part of our language.

About the time of the Revolutionary War, the Continental Congress authorized the printing and use of paper money, but most people did not want to accept it. Critics claimed the small pieces of paper were only good as leg and knee bandages, and that's how the Continental Currency notes got the nickname, "shin plasters."

Uncle Sam was not alone in producing currency in the 1800s. During the mid to late nineteenth century, many banks produced and used their own paper money, some of which eventually was about as worthless as those shin plasters. Between 1863 and 1928, more than 13,000 private banks were granted special charters to issue their own paper money. Earlier, some banks and merchants issued rather odd denominations, such as $3 bills, and even denominations of $7.50 and $15. These notes are collected by many people today.

Because there was massive hoarding of copper, silver and gold coins during the Civil War, the U.S. Congress permitted private banks to issue money under the National Currency Act of Feb. 25, 1863, and the National Banking Act of June 3, 1864. (Many merchants began issuing their own copper pieces because of the severe coin shortages, but that's another story involving Civil War and merchants' tokens. See chapter 19.)

The thousands of different kinds of paper money produced by the various banks up until 1935, when the laws were repealed and only the federal government again was authorized to issue currency, are known as National Bank Notes, and usually are referred to by collectors as "Nationals." Some collectors assemble sets of "nationals" by denomination, by bank, by city, by state, or by the signatures on the notes. Several survey respondents suggested starting a collection of Nationals from your own home state.

It is impossible to obtain "one of everything" because some examples are either unique, or apparently non-existent. Records may indicate certain types of notes were printed and issued, but no remaining examples are known today. Still, collectors spend happy hours hunting for these items, and now and then another new specimen is discovered.

The familiar pieces of currency we use today (and often struggle to hang on to) were first introduced in 1929, although some carry the currency series date of 1928. Before then some of the notes were similar in design to our current currency, but they were considerably larger in size. Often these big notes were called "horse blankets," but they weren't THAT large.

The detailed portraits and scenes (vignettes) depicted on the paper money of the nineteenth and early twentieth centuries range from unusual to superb pieces of art. Some notes of the late 1800s have drawings of Seated Liberty design coins; those were the kinds of coins in circulation at the time. Others portray various scenes of Americana from pioneer families to symbolic representations of Liberty, History, and Science.

The American Bank Note Company of New York (ABNCo.) produced many of the colorful paper money on behalf of banks during the nineteenth century. Over its 200 year history, ABNCo. has serviced over seventy countries with paper money, stock certificates, bonds, travelers' checks and other security documents. The company recognizes the collector interest in its products, especially the vignettes produced by master engravers. "Many of these delicately engraved vignettes are representative of American life during the nineteenth century as seen through the artistic eye of the engraver. The vignettes depict a wide variety of subjects which include American Indians, railroads, sailing ships, family life, architecture, presidents and other notables in the

An example of the American Bank Note Company vignettes that captured life in nineteenth century America. *(Photo courtesy ABNCo.)*

financial worlds, and many more," explained an ABNCo. press release.

(The letterhead for that press release was superbly produced by intaglio printing, the design was boldly raised so you could feel it by gently running your fingers across it!)

All paper money issued by the United States government since the 1860s is still redeemable at face value. (The "Trade Dollar" silver coins issued from 1873 to 1885 were de-monetized and for years they actually were worth less than their face value of one dollar. Now, of course, as collectors' items they range in value from around $75 each for well-worn examples of common date pieces to more than $100,000 for a very rare 1885 proof Trade Dollar.) Even though all this paper money since the 1860s can be redeemed for face value, they usually are worth considerably more as numismatic items. Thomas Gittings, senior research economist at the Federal Reserve Bank of Chicago and the bank's museum curator, reports that each year the bank redeems several hundred dollars worth of gold certificate notes at face value. Usually, these are crumpled, very worn common notes that have virtually no collectors value. However, Dr. Gittings tells the heartbreaking story of how some crisp, uncirculated specimens were brought to the bank by heirs of the paper money's recently-deceased owner. These valuable notes were exchanged at face value for new bills. Unfortunately, the bank clerks then followed the rule book and sent the gold certificates to be destroyed, rather than exercising the option of placing them in the bank's museum. Those notes certainly would have been worth more than their weight in gold.

Silver certificate and gold certificate notes, despite the claims printed on their faces, no longer can be exchanged for silver or gold bullion; however, Uncle Sam gladly will exchange them for new bills.

After the BEP has printed both sides of a sheet of paper money, the sheets may remain in storage until needed. When the notes are ready to be distributed through the Federal Reserve Bank system, the notes go through the presses a third time and the serial numbers and Federal Reserve Bank district are added to the face. That's why, now and then, you find errors with the serial numbers printed upside down or on the back; the sheet of paper was incorrectly fed into the printing press. Very rarely a sheet of paper money is printed with one denomination on the face and a different denomination on the back.

Notes with a star in the serial number indicate something may have gone wrong in the printing process. The Federal Reserve Bank of Atlanta explains it this way in the booklet, *Fundamental Facts About United States Money:*

"If a note is damaged in the process of printing, it is replaced with a 'star' note. Star notes are made up with independent runs of serial numbers and are exactly like the notes they replace, except that a star is substituted for one of the serial letters."

Prominent paper money specialist John Wilson of Wisconsin recommends assembling a type set of small-sized fractional currency of the 1860s and 1870s with the denominations of 3, 5, 10, 15, 25, and 50 cent notes. Many of these notes can be purchased for less than $100 each even in Crisp Uncirculated (CU) condition, and many can be obtained for less than $20 in Extremely Fine grade. These fractional notes originally were produced because of the acute hoarding of copper and silver coins during the Civil War. Between August 1862, and April 1876, nearly $370 million worth of these small bills were printed, yet it is estimated that less than $500,000 worth remains unredeemed or undestroyed.

As with many areas of rare coins, assembling a fine collection of currency can be easy or a lengthy hunt, but it also can be plenty of fun. You can acquire many colorful items at quite reasonable costs—not including the rare error notes printed ten dollars on one side and twenty dollars on the other. Next time you handle a piece of paper money, whether it is a crisp new specimen or a battered old rag, pause a moment to—take note.

Obverse

Reverse

Despite a few modest scrapes and gouges, this high quality 1793 Chain cent would attract an enthusiastic crowd at any meeting of the Early American Coppers group. *(Photos by James A. Simek)*

CHAPTER TWELVE

Large Cents and Half Cents

"Gone are the days. . . ."

-Harry E. Salyards-

Some teachers place stars on their young students' outstanding papers. School teacher Ralph Dintruff found stars on a corroded copper coin and he's the one who learned a valuable lesson.

Dintruff, a New York state school teacher, was visiting a coin shop in Maryland in April 1987, and purchased an assortment of seven different copper pieces for $33. One of the coins is worth thousands of dollars. Now that's a valuable lesson outside the classroom!

Dintruff discovered one of the approximately fifty known specimens of the 1794 U.S. large cent struck with ninety-four tiny stars almost hidden in the design around the denticles on the reverse. Copper coin specialists list this

as a Sheldon variety number 48 (S-48), named after the late
Dr. William H. Sheldon who wrote a delightful book about
early U.S. large cents in 1958, *Penny Whimsy.*

Even though the teacher's coin was "covered with crud,"
according to large cent researcher Pete Smith of Minnesota,
there was a visible trace of stars on the reverse indicating it is
one of the very rare specimens. The reason for the tiny,
five-pointed stars is not known, although there is speculation
a mint employee with little else to do became "creative." One
of the few known examples of his artwork was discovered by
Dintruff in a Maryland coin shop.

"The coin has suffered from burial, immersion, and/or
other poor storage conditions. Grade is probably AG-3. It
definitely fits the definition of 'worse than scudzy,'" Smith
wrote in *Penny-Wise*, the publication of the Early American
Coppers club.

Despite the crud and corrosion the coin is worth about
$3,000, perhaps more, and it only cost Dintruff about $4.75
because it was just one of seven items he purchased for a
combined total of $33.

If numismatics has an elite corps it surely includes
members of Early American Coppers (EAC). They don't act
"elitist," but the 1,400 members of this non-profit group are
devoted (perhaps enslaved might be an appropriate word) to
the study and joy of early United States copper coins. While
the emphasis seems to be on large cents from 1793 to 1814,
collectors of later dates, half-cents, and Colonial era copper
are most welcome. EAC members look at the Who, What,
Where, When, Why, and How of early American copper
coinage. They share their findings in a semi-scholarly, yet
lively newsletter, *Penny-Wise*, which frequently prints an-
nouncements involving discovery of new die varieties. For
more information on EAC, see chapter 23.

The name *Penny-Wise* comes from Dr. Sheldon's book,
Penny Whimsy, the Bible of early American copper. Another
cherished work is *United States Copper Cents* authored in 1944
by H.R. Newcomb. Together, they provide the basic founda-
tion for the study of U.S. large cents struck from 1793 to 1857.

The first United States one cent denomination coins (there actually is no official designation "penny" in U.S. coinage) are slightly larger in size and more than twice as heavy in weight than modern quarter dollars. The phrase, "A penny for your thoughts," had real meaning then. These are big coins and had considerably more purchasing power than today's one cent pieces. The designs of early large cents changed often; sometimes a major alteration at the request of mint officials and others, sometimes just slight differences between one newly-made die and another with essentially the "same" designs on them. U.S. large cents have a strong collector appeal, and recently have attracted the attention of others who earlier had overlooked and even scorned this field.

The editor of *Penny-Wise*, Harry E. Salyards, offers this self-described "inadequate and tangential" explanation of why early copper coins are so popular. "The profound simplicity of the designs, 'Liberty'—'United States of America'—'1794,' define a condition, a place, and a time in a straightforward manner which we've never surpassed."

When it comes to large cents, you quickly learn it is not just gem quality coins that attract attention. In many cases, when a particular coin becomes available in nearly any condition there are eager buyers. The popular 1793 Chain cent is an excellent example. There are many more buyers than there are available specimens of this rare coin. Only 36,103 were minted before the chain design on the reverse was changed to a wreath because there were complaints the linked chains were symbolic of slavery. Actually, the links in the chain were intended to symbolize the unity of the young colonies.

Chain cents have performed well over the past decade, especially in lower grades. In very worn, About Good condition (AG-3), they've increased from around $300 to $350 each in 1980 to around $1,200 each now. In Extremely Fine grade (XF-40) they've jumped from around $8,000 to $10,000 each in 1980 to about $17,500 to $20,000—if you can locate a specimen in that grade.

Obverse   Reverse

Another example of an early large cent, a 1795 Liberty Cap type. The Draped Bust type also was struck that year. *(Photos by James A. Simek)*

There are many major types of large cents—Chain, Draped Bust, Classic Head, and so on. Within those types are scores of interesting varieties, some with colorful names to describe Miss Liberty's appearance; Booby Head, Silly Head, and Jefferson Head because Miss Liberty bears a resemblence to Thomas Jefferson (although the 1795 Jefferson Head large cent is not considered a regular mint issue). Large cent specialists avidly study these, often carrying to coin shows well-read copies of their Sheldon and Newcomb books, searching for elusive rarities, such as the 1794 S-48 starred reverse variety mentioned above. They can still be found.

In the spring of 1990, a dealer sent several coins to ANACS to be authenticated and encapsulated prior to being placed in a major auction. He insured one of the coins for several hundred dollars, but ANACS Director Leonard Albrecht telephoned the customer suggesting he might want ANACS to insure that coin for $10,000 when they returned it to him. Yes, it was a starred reverse variety large cent, although the owner thought it was "only" a decent quality "regular" 1794 cent when he submitted it to ANACS for slabbing. The coin was graded VF-20 and sold for $19,800 (including the 10 percent buyer's fee) at Auction '90, one of the biggest numismatic events of the year.

Starting in the late 1980s the U.S. rare coin market started discovering early American copper. *Penny-Wise* Editor Salyards described EAC's 1990 convention auction as "skyrocketing prices for nice material. . . . The supply is increasingly thin. Gone are the days when Jack Beymer (a well-known copper coin specialist dealer) had two dozen Chain cents to lay out, side-by-side, in his case (twenty-three, to be exact, at EAC '82). . . ."

EAC member Peter Boisvert of Milford, Massachusetts, says the "better varieties" of large cents have experienced "phenomenal growth."

If you think a penny won't buy much these days, how about a half cent? Although certainly not the smallest sized coin struck by the United States, the half cent is the smallest denomination. The first pieces were struck in 1793—the same year large cent production began—and the last half cents were produced by the mint in 1857—the same year large cent production stopped. Often described by large cent collectors as the "little sisters," half cents have attracted the attention of many numismatists who are delighted with small copper coins bearing the denomination "1/200" of a dollar.

Because of the small denomination, half cents were frequently used in the early years of their production. Many collectors are thrilled to locate even a Very Fine or Extremely Fine specimen of some dates, such as 1802.

Die varieties of these coins usually are classified by either "B" or "C" numbers, the B stands for Walter Breen, the C for Roger S. Cohen, Jr. That makes sense because the two basic reference books on half cents are *Walter Breen's Encyclopedia of United States Half Cents 1793–1857* and *American Half Cents: the "Little Half Sisters,"* written by Roger S. Cohen, Jr. Often, specialists will list a particular coin by both Breen and Cohen variety numbers, for example, the 1795 Breen variety, B-6c, is also known as Cohen variety, C-6a. It can get a little confusing, but with a nearby copy of one or the other

Obverse   Reverse

From the first year of the "little sisters" issue, a choice quality 1793 half cent. *(Photos by James A. Simek)*

reference book the beginning half cent collector will quickly learn the terminology.

Collector Ralph C. Langham of Connecticut, national coordinator of the ANA's network of club and district representatives (true hobby ambassadors!), placed 1793 large cents and half cents as numbers one and two on his survey list, and later also suggested any VF/XF Sheldon variety, early date large cents.

Pat Davis of California had proof half cents high on the survey list. Cincinnati dealer Mark Mendelson placed proof half cents and circulation strikes in MS-64 or better grade first on his list. David Fanning, Mendelson's colleague at Fountain Square Stamp and Coin Company, likes half cents in MS-64 grade or better, early large cents in at least MS-63, and later date large cents in MS-65 grade or better. Dean Schmidt listed "Classic Large Cent, MS-64 and better," while Q. David Bowers placed at the top of his list of specific coins, "U.S. large cents, 1816 to 1857, Extremely Fine to MS-60." (Dave also strongly recommends "a nice numismatic library." See chapter 23.)

Jacksonville, Arkansas, dealer Robert T. McIntire likes most any American copper coins of 1795 to 1857 in XF-45 grade or better.

In determining the value of a choice copper coin, color is a crucial factor. In general, the redder the better, although many large cent specialists would be thrilled to acquire a lovely chocolate colored specimen of a Chain cent or other rare date or variety. Even for common date large cents of the 1850s, a little natural mint color adds a lot of value. For example, in certified (slabbed) MS-64 grade, a brown coin might sell for, say, $500, but with red and brown coloring it could be priced at $675. A red specimen graded MS-64 would sell for perhaps $1,200 or more.

Here is the ANACS criteria for describing copper coins as red, red & brown (R&B), and brown.

RED—Copper

1. The (full) RED designation will ONLY be applied to those copper coins which display a complete and uniform, original "red" color over their entire surface. Hues may vary from deep red to golden red, but the key is uniform and being in the red color range.

2. Coins with streaks, stains, toning, fingerprints, carbon spots visible without magnification or any characteristic other than a totally uniform red surface will be downgraded to RED & BROWN.

3. The RED designation will apply only to those coins with a final grade of MS-60 and above or PF-60 and above.

RED & BROWN—Copper

1. The RED & BROWN designation applies to a wide range of copper color schemes. At the top end, it may mean "mostly" red with hints of brown or some of the problems previously mentioned. At the bottom end, it would mean

mostly brown with noticeable hints or highlights of some red hue. The latter defines the minimum guidelines.

2. The RED & BROWN designation will apply only to those coins with a final grade of MS-60 and above or PF-60 and above.

BROWN—Copper
1. The BROWN designation applies to copper coins which display a complete "brown" color over their entire surface. Hues may vary from chocolate to olive and may be mixed. The key here is that no noticeable trace of red hue is evident on the coin.

2. The BROWN designation will apply only to those coins with a final grade of MS-60 or above or PF-60 or above.

Obverse

Reverse

The mint superintendent's daughter did not spend this specimen of the 1894-S Barber dime, it is the finest known example. *(Photos by James A. Simek)*

CHAPTER THIRTEEN

Barber Coinage

"There is still a lot to be discovered in

the series."

-Steven Epstein-

It is rare today to find a rare coin in circulation. If you locate a scarce date or mintmark, chances are good either someone finally broke open an old piggy bank or, unfortunately for the victim, someone's coin collection was stolen and the thief spent at least some of the items as pocket change. One of the most famous circulation finds in U.S. coin collecting history involves a Barber dime.

Although some U.S. coins are known as "Flowing Hair, Coiled Hair, and Braided Hair" designs, Barber dimes have nothing to do with hair styles. Named after the then Chief Engraver of the U.S. Mint, Charles Barber, the term Barber coinage generally refers to the dimes, quarters and half dollars issued starting in 1892. Barber coins are popular enough to have their own fan club, the Barber Coin Collectors Society (see below and chapter 23).

An unidentified person, presumably in California, was the first to discover an exceptionally rare 1894-S dime that had been placed into circulation by the daughter of the San Francisco Mint's Director, J. Daggett. Only twenty-four dimes were struck at the San Francisco Mint in 1894. The specific reason for the tiny mintage is still subject to speculation, debate, and controversy. Some claim the Mint Director commanded the coinage of $2.40 in dimes just to balance out the year's total production with an even number. If so, why strike only proof dimes?

Another theory is that a prominent San Francisco banker asked his friend, Mint Director Daggett, to make some of these coins for himself and a group of influential colleagues.

Three of the 1894-S dimes were given by Daggett to his young daughter, Hallie, with instructions that she keep them until she was much older because they would be valuable. She did keep two of them for years, but she spent one of the dimes while still a child. She used it to purchase a dish of ice cream.

One of the known specimens of the 1894-S dime is only in Good condition, an obvious victim of considerable circulation. Perhaps that is the dime used by young Miss Daggett to buy ice cream, and eventually found in pocket change by an astute collector who realized the coin could buy more than just 31 flavors.

That's just one of the fascinating aspects of Barber coins.

In January 1989, collector Steve Epstein of Akron, Ohio, met with various hobby leaders attending the annual Florida United Numismatists (appropriately named, FUN) convention, and they formed the Barber Coin Collectors Society. About a year later, in a *Coin World* interview with hobby writer William Atkinson, Epstein explained that he loves the Barber coinage series. "They are relatively easy to grade once you know what you're doing, and it is really difficult to find nice Extremely Fine and About Uncirculated examples with sufficient eye appeal. That makes the series a challenge to collect," he explained.

Among the approximately 400 members of the club, Epstein says the largest number of Barber Coin Collectors Society members specialize in dimes (1892 to 1916), followed in popularity by Barber quarters (1892 to 1916), and a few specialize in Barber halves (1892 to 1915). Interestingly, the half dollar series actually has the fewest rarities, and therefore is easier to assemble as an entire set in circulated grades.

"There is still a lot to be discovered in the [entire Barber coinage] series," he said. "Some dates are very common in low grades, rare in Extremely Fine or About Uncirculated, and then common again in Uncirculated. A lot of people don't know this, and even many dealers sell very rare coins inexpensively. The 1911-D Barber quarter, for example, is extremely difficult to locate in XF or AU with any kind of eye appeal."

For more information about this specialty club, write to Barber Coin Collectors Society, P.O. Box 5353, Akron, Ohio 44313. Club dues are ten dollars per year, and that includes a subscription to the society's quarterly journal.

Among the survey's recommendations for Barber coinage was Cincinnati dealer David Fanning's suggestion to consider Barber quarters in MS-65 and better condition. A collector wrote "any slabbed Barber coins in MS-65 or higher for their beauty and value." Prominent Texas collector Lyman C. Bartee listed both Barber quarters and half dollars AU quality or better and proof, while South Laguna, California, dealer Mike Kliman recommended proof Barber dimes. Bruce R. Longyear of Boston's J.J. Teaparty Coin Company placed "all better date, rare or scarce" XF or better Barber coins among his recommendations, emphasizing you should purchase "only original, uncleaned, attractive examples" of those or any other coins.

Gainesville, Florida, dealer Roger P. Bryan points out relatively few Barber quarters have been certified as Proof-66 and thinks these could be one of the top numismatic investments. Another survey participant encourages collectors to seek out MS-63 or better Barber coinage with a low premium/date-scarcity ratio. With a little detective work you can find high grade, lower mintage coins that sell for close to the same amount as common dates of the same grade. This is true for many coinage series, not just Barber.

In the Barber dime, quarter and half dollar series, coins from the New Orleans Mint (mintmark "O") often appear weakly struck.

Obverse

Reverse

The key coin to the Indian Head cent series, the 1877. This sharply struck piece clearly shows full diamond designs in the headdress ribbon. *(Photos by James A. Simek)*

CHAPTER FOURTEEN

Indian Head Cents

"An All-American coin."

- John Iddings -

Just about every year, New York attorney, collector, and American Numismatic Association Governor David L. Ganz lists Indian Head cents among his year-end predictions for rare coin investments. And, just about every year in his annual *COINage* magazine prediction article, Ganz admits the previous year's forecast about Indian Head cents exploding in value did not become reality. Yet, Ganz believes these coins have tremendous potential, and common date, superb quality, red color, Indian Head cents traded hands in 1990 in excess of $3,000 with even higher prices for some pieces at auction.

Indian Head cents were struck for circulation between 1859 and 1909. Numismatic writer John Iddings once described these as ". . . an All-American coin that weathered the Civil War and spanned the days of the Wild West." Now that's a lot of history for a little coin. According to the *Red Book*, the obverse is supposed to represent an Indian Princess. Numismatic researcher Walter Breen found evidence that coin designer James B. Longacre used a statue of the goddess Venus as his model.

Indian Head cents were produced in two thicknesses with two different metal compositions, copper-nickel and bronze. There are two major varieties of Indian Cents made of copper-nickel; without a shield above the wreath on the reverse, 1859 only, and with the shield, 1860 to 1864. Many of these coins were not sharply struck, especially those made of copper-nickel. A key feature to examine for sharpness of strike is the tiny diamond designs in the ribbons of the Indian's headdress. If they are full and sharp, the coin will have a higher value.

Starting in 1864, the coin's weight was reduced and it was made in bronze, 95 percent copper and 5 percent tin. Also in 1864, Longacre added the initial "L" hidden in a headdress ribbon. Most cents of that particular year do not contain the engraver's initial, those that do are scarce and worth considerably more than coins without the lone letter. This is an example of collectors spending time looking for an "L" of a coin.

The Indian Head cent is a coinage series that can be completed by most any collector because the scarce dates are not so scarce as to be impossible to locate. The two most valuable coins in the Indian Head cent series are the 1877, valued at about $225 in Good, and the 1909-S, valued at about $100 in the same grade. Common date coins of the late 1880s and early 1900s can be purchased for less than $100 even in red color MS-63 condition. Think about that. A century old coin, with an interesting, historic design, still exhibiting its original red color, and costing less $100, perhaps even less than $75. One of these days, the prediction of David Ganz will become reality.

Many survey respondents who listed Indian Head cents

suggested assembling an entire set in XF/AU condition. Lincoln cent specialist Virg Marshall III of Wymore, Nebraska, ("The Penny Merchant") put Indian Head cents at the top of his survey. He recommended coins between 1859 and 1879 in the range of Very Fine to About Uncirculated. Another respondent suggested any Indian Cents in VG to XF grade to start a collection.

Berwyn, Illinois, dealer Mitchell Mattrey suggested Indian Head cents in Uncirculated grades, "Unc. or better." Lexington, Kentucky, dealer Tom Mulvaney recommended Mint State or proof Indian Head cents that are red and unspotted. This focuses on two important eye appeal factors; the desirable color of the copper coin (see chapter 12), and the total lack of any distracting carbon spots that have infected so many otherwise choice-colored copper coins. There is considerable speculation and hope that slabbing will preserve high quality copper coins and prevent them from future environmental contamination. Slabs are still relatively new, so it may be decades before we learn just how well those sealed plastic holders are protecting the luster and surfaces of today's gems.

Respected silver dollar specialist Steven L. Contursi of Newport Beach, California, (see chapter 4) placed red "Indian Cents in PR-65" at the top of his list, scarce coins that can be obtained for less than $800 even in this high quality. However, the price probably will be double that amount or more if you locate a red PR-66 specimen.

Obverse

Reverse

Among the European coins recommended in the survey are the proof 20 Mark gold German coins of 1871 to 1914. *(Photos by James A. Simek)*

CHAPTER FIFTEEN

European Coinage

"No slabs . . . !"

- *Anonymous* -

Although no major grading service is slabbing ancient coins (chapter 10), several do offer authentication, certification, and encapsulation of non-U.S. coins from the 1800s and after. PCGS is evaluating certain Canadian, British, German, Japanese and Swiss coins. Interestingly, while these slabbed world coins have found some acceptance in the United States, they often have encountered resistance in their home countries. Time will tell.

One expert on European coinage, who requested anonymity for the survey, warned, "Foreign coins should NOT be bought from U.S. dealers who stock *only* "GEM" foreign coins: The price paid [by the customers] will be too high in relation to real market value in the country of origin. No slabs, either!"

Non-U.S. numismatic items usually are referred to as "world" coins and currency, not "foreign." While many different world coin items were suggested in the survey, the majority of non-U.S. items fell under the category, "European coinage." There are oh-so-many potential areas of collecting in this vast field. There literally are thousands of possible starting places for anyone thinking about this popular area of numismatics. Survey respondents occasionally listed their specific suggestions, and many times they included German coins.

When collectors talk about "German coins" they can be discussing literally thousands of varieties dating back literally a thousand years. The German Empire goes back to the year 843 A.D. and the Treaty of Verdun. Before then, many coins were struck in and for the area of "Germany" under the Holy Roman Empire. So, even though today we may think of the recently divided and reunited country (formerly East and West Germany) only in modern, post World War Two terms, there is a lengthy and rich numismatic heritage that dates back to ancient times.

Adding even more delight—and often a bit of confusion —for collectors are the various coinages of the German States. By the mid-1600s there were an estimated 1,800 different states that made up the area known as Germany. *The Standard Catalog of World Coins,* a superb annual reference work that lists more than 75,000 types of coins struck over the last 230 or so years (see chapter 23), tracks 61 numismatically important German States from Aaschen to Wurzburg.

The "modern" German Empire was founded in 1871 and its 26 kingdoms, grand duchies, duchies, principalities, free states, and provinces generally were permitted to issue their own coins. Each of these coins has a story to tell. Some of the denominations may seem strange to collectors just getting started. "Pfennig" and "Thaler" perhaps are familiar; they sound like "penny" and "dollar." But how about Heller? Or,

Groschen and Mariengroschen? Those are just three of the interesting denomination designations for interesting coins. There are dozens of possible mintmarks on the coins, too. Bamberg, Frankfurt, Hamburg, Dresden, Hannover, Brunswick, Breslau, and Munich are just a few of the towns were coins were struck.

There are many ways to collect German coins. Naturally, one of the most popular is to collect by state, concentrating on different denominations, dates, and mintmarks from one or more specific German states. Another delightful way is to pick a particular year and try to obtain one coin from each state minted with that date on it. You also can collect by denomination, again acquiring coins of the same denomination from the different states. Or, just collect whatever you find interesting.

Here's the best part. German coins, and most coins of the world, are downright cheap compared to United States coins of comparable years, sizes, and conditions. You can find many items struck in the 1700s for $10 to $25. Even higher grade specimens often are comparatively cheap to U.S. issues of the same years. Sure, there also are very rare, expensive German coins.

Marc Emory who works in Germany for Dallas' Heritage Rare Coins recommends common types of Proof-65 or better German 20 Mark gold coins of 1871 to 1914, and Proof-65 or better English gold sovereigns of 1887 and 1893. Emory noted that in European numismatic terminology, "Uncirculated" often is described with the French phrase, Fleur de Coin (FDC).

Interestingly, one of the foremost numismatic researchers of United States coinage, Robert W. Julian of Indiana, recommends purchasing nineteenth and twentieth century European silver crowns. (He also suggests putting together U.S. type sets and buying pre-1954 U.S. commemorative coins.)

Chicago collector Pete Jorstad, C.P.A., thinks British Royal Mint proof sets represent a "standard of excellence," and are among the items that could give someone a good start in collecting European coinage. Colorado collector

Obverse   Reverse

One of the most beautiful silver coins of Great Britain, the 1847 "Gothic Crown" depicting a young Queen Victoria. *(Photos by James A. Simek)*

William F. Spengler thinks medieval English and other European coins provide both "historical connections with American culture, and value," and are among the items giving an alternative collecting view to what Spengler calls "the bags, rolls and slabs guys."

Norman Applebaum of M. Louis Teller Numismatic Company, Encino, California, recommended "low mintage, choice condition commemorative foreign gold." Hackensack, New Jersey, dealer Andy Lustig, well-known in the field of U.S. pattern and territorial coinage, placed English hammered silver and gold coins second on his survey list. (He did recommend U.S. territorial gold, too, along with 1792 U.S. pattern coinage; both utterly fascinating and usually expensive.)

Monterey Park, California, dealer Frank Draskovic listed two potential areas of European coinage on his survey sheet: "World Crowns and Thalers 1500 to 1800, XF or better; World Crowns and Minors 1800 to 1940, Choice Unc." He also likes "scarce and rare world paper money, XF or better." Ira M. Goldberg of Superior Stamp and Coin Company, Beverly Hills, California, likes "European gold coins from popular

Western countries, eighteenth and nineteenth centuries, in Choice Brilliant Uncirculated condition."

World coin specialist Steve Eyer of Mt. Zion, Illinois, only recommended Swiss Shooting Thalers of 1984 to 1990, popular silver and gold coins struck starting in the 1840s that honor marksmanship. "They always go up," he wrote on his survey. "I don't know of others that go up without fail."

Other recommendations from dealers and collectors included these: "Choice minors and crowns of the Victorian era." "Foreign proof gold at melt value plus 5 percent." "Gem BU, pre-1910 foreign coins in MS-65 or better, when reasonable [in price]." "All foreign coins of Western Europe and British colonies dated before 1900 in MS-63 to 65."

When it comes to coinage of the European continent, you have a world of choices.

Obverse

Reverse

Obverse

Reverse

The coin that caused a scandal: The 1917 bare breasted Standing Liberty quarter and an example from 1919 of how Miss Liberty was covered up. Notice there also are changes on the reverse between the Variety I and Variety II designs. *(Photos by James A. Simek)*

CHAPTER SIXTEEN

Standing Liberty Quarters

"... truly a collectors' series."

-J.H. Cline-

Forget the savings & loan industry crisis. Step aside Watergate. The introduction of the Standing Liberty quarters in 1916 produced a government scandal that evoked a nationwide public outcry. The coin design shows Miss Liberty with a virtually bare right breast!

The Standing Liberty quarters were designed by famous architect, engraver, and sculptor Hermon Atkins MacNeil. The Commission of Fine Arts and the U.S. Treasury Department jointly agreed that MacNeil's proposed design would replace the quarter designed by Charles Barber that had been circulating since 1892. President Theodore Roosevelt, who exerted direct influence on introduction of the beautiful $20 gold piece designed by Augustus Saint-Gaudens (chapter 9), also wanted the Barber coinage replaced because he thought it lacked adequate artistic merit.

So, MacNeil's new quarter dollar design was approved in May 1916, and went into circulation later that year. The *Red Book* briefly refers to the controversy over the semi-nude Miss Liberty as "public resentment."

In 1917, at the request of the Mint, MacNeil modified both the obverse and reverse, covering Miss Liberty's exposed breast and changing the arrangement of stars around and under the eagle. Some critics complained the eagle looked more like the body of a dove with eagle's wings and a hawk's beak, but MacNeil defended his rendition of the bird. There are both Variety I (exposed breast) and Variety II (covered breast) 1917 quarters from the Philadelphia, Denver and San Francisco mints. The 1916 pieces only were struck at Philadelphia.

Another design change was made in 1925. The date on the bottom of the coin's obverse was slightly "recessed," so it would not be raised as high and so easily worn down. The date is contained in the pedestal on which Miss Liberty, clothed or partially exposed, stands.

One characteristic of a fully struck Standing Liberty quarter is the amount of design showing on Miss Liberty's head. Quarters described as "FH" indicate Full Head. Even with a Full Head, other parts of the design may show weakness, for example, around the shield and Miss Liberty's knees. This lovely coinage series can be difficult to accurately grade. I've even heard several veteran dealers claim that virtually all Uncirculated Standing Liberty quarters show some "rub" on the knees.

Long-time Kansas City, Missouri, dealer W. L. "Dutch" Rohning of Mid-Continent Coins, Inc., thinks the Standing Liberty quarter series is an excellent place for collectors to start. *Chicago Tribune* coin columnist Roger Boye calls it "my favorite series" and recommends buying them in Uncirculated condition and higher grades. J.H. Cline of Palm Harbor, Florida, a dealer specializing in this coinage series and author of the book, *Standing Liberty Quarters*, says these coins are "truly a collectors' series. It is a series that has a lot of merit going for it." His specific date and mintmark recommendations include "most any Standing Liberty quarter in Mint State 65 and up," all 1916 (type one variety) pieces in XF or higher, as well as 1919 Denver and San Francisco mintmarked with or without full heads in MS-63/65 grade, and all 1927-S quarters in Uncirculated grades. While there is considerable attention on Mint State specimens, Cline encourages buyers also to look for Full Head coins in AU condition. That's a recommendation shared by Jim Beasley of Tilden Coin Company in Orlando, Florida.

Connecticut collector Ralph C. Langham encourages collectors to find gem quality 1921, 1923-S, and 1927-S quarters. Former PNG President Leon Hendrickson of Winchester, Indiana, suggests any MS-63 specimen of a Variety II Standing Liberty quarter. Several other survey respondents recommended MS-65 or better.

Arizona dealer Elliot S. Goldman wishes collectors "happy hunting" trying to locate a 1927-S quarter in AU or better grade. He also likes 1916 Standing Liberty quarters in Very Fine condition or better. Dallas dealer Jim Halperin listed 1926-S in MS-63, a rather low mintage (2.7 million) coin that usually can be obtained in that condition for not much more than the cost of a "common" Standing Liberty quarter of comparable grade.

There is a major overdate variety in the Standing Liberty quarter series, 1918/7-S, a rare coin in Uncirculated condition. Jeffrey F. Bernberg of Rare Coin Company of America in Willowbrook, Illinois, recommended this well-known error coin in a certified (slabbed) MS-61 or MS-62 grade.

ANACS uses the following criteria for the designation Full Head on Variety I Standing Liberty quarters.

1. The coin will exhibit all other criteria normally required for "sharply struck," with no visible weakness

throughout the design on either side. (Obverse—shield, drapery, knee, date. Reverse—eagle's details.)

2. Hair details must be well defined; hairline along face must be raised and complete.

3. The eyebrow must be visible; cheek must be rounded.

4. The Full Head designation will be applied only to those coins with a final grade of MS-60 or above.

The criteria for Full Head designation for Variety II Standing Liberty quarters adds a few more guidelines.

1. Criteria for the Variety I quarter also applies.

2. The hairline along Liberty's brow and face must be complete and uninterrupted.

3. The three leaves in the hair must be well defined and complete.

4. The small indentation at Liberty's ear must be visible.

5. The Full Head designation will be applied only to those coins with a final grade of MS-60 or above.

Specialist J.H. Cline points out that 1916 Standing Liberty quarters usually are not struck as fully as 1917 Variety I specimens. When looking for Full Head features, Cline warns: "The worst 1917s usually are better than the best 1916s."

For information on obtaining a copy of his book, *Standing Liberty Quarters (revised)*, write to J.H. Cline, P.O. Box 1180, Palm Harbor, Florida 34273.

Obverse

Reverse

From its first year of issue, a 1932 Washington quarter with a typically weak strike of the motto, IN GOD WE TRUST. *(Photos by James A. Simek)*

CHAPTER SEVENTEEN

Washington Quarters

"The use of knowledge is power."

- James A. Simek -

Would you like to pay only about $15 for a $200 coin? Don't bother to respond, the answer is obvious. But don't reach for your wallet, yet; instead, reach for your magnifying glass and get ready for a hunting expedition. Your prey will be seldom-recognized Washington quarter doubled-die varieties, and with a little luck and a lot of patience you'll be rewarded with the opportunity to buy a $200 coin for around $15. But, only if you know what to look for.

"You may be familiar with the expression, 'Knowledge is power.' Yet, that's not really correct. The proper way of saying it should be, 'The *use* of knowledge is power," explains dealer James A. Simek of NumisGraphics in Westchester,

Illinois. Simek is an expert on U.S. quarter dollars and has advantageously used his knowledge many times. One of those occasions was when he saw a 1934 doubled-die Washington quarter in AU condition priced at $3, a fair price at the time for a "regular" quarter in that grade. However, this specimen exhibited doubling in the motto, IN GOD WE TRUST, prominently visible under low power magnification. It is similar to the kind of doubling found on the popular 1955 and 1972 doubled-die Lincoln cents. It looks like one part of the design closely stamped over itself. Simek purchased the 1934 quarter for $3 and later sold it for $150 to another dealer specializing in error coins. Today, that same coin would be worth at least $200, while a "regular" 1934 Washington quarter in AU grade would sell for about $15.

"We use our knowledge in our jobs or in school, at least we should. If we take that one step further and use knowledge in our hobby, numismatics, we may find it makes things more profitable, more enjoyable, more interesting. I'm not saying that use of knowledge will allow us to reap only monetary rewards, but in today's marketplace where the hobby is becoming more expensive to pursue, the monetary implications are becoming more important," Simek said.

In the *Red Book*'s section on Washington quarters, there are three listings for varieties of 1934 Philadelphia quarters: The Light Motto, also known as the Type of 1932 (because the IN GOD WE TRUST motto did not strike up very well in the first year of issue and Mint officials decided changes were needed to improve its weak appearance); Heavy Motto or Type of 1936 (where the motto is bolder); and the 1934 doubled-die mentioned at the beginning of this chapter.

Simek explains: "Not listed in the *Red Book*, but still a major variety of 1934 quarter, is the Type of 1935. You can determine this variety by looking at the letter 'W' in the word 'WE.' In your mind, draw an imaginary line across the top letters in the motto. If the mid-point in the center of the 'W' does not extend above the line, that's a Type of 1935. If it extends above the imaginary line, then it's a Type of 1936. Those are just some of the varieties of early Washington quarters."

These quarters were first struck in 1932 to commemorate the bicentennial of President George Washington's birth. No coins dated 1933 were produced, but since 1934 the Father of Our Country annually has appeared on United States quarter dollars. Washington quarters may seem "common" if the definition of common means they are readily available from most dealers. However, as a coinage series, they are not common; you cannot complete a set by searching through pocket change because most everything struck before 1965 no longer is in circulation. The silver coins have vanished from cash registers, except for the occasional busted piggy bank specimens or, horrors! stolen coins that are placed in circulation by a thief.

Even if Washington quarters are viewed by many people as "common," there still are rarities in the series, such as the 1932-D and 1932-S with mintages of only 436,800 and 408,000 respectively, and there still are bargains to be found. One such bargain is locating the kind of major variety Simek discovered in another dealer's stock.

Another surprising bargain may be found by comparing the overall scarcity of low mintage, high grade silver Washington quarters with the prices of other numismatic items. A few researchers have speculated that sharply struck, gem quality clad coinage, such as Washington quarters minted after 1964 and composed of copper and nickel, could become future rarities. Apparently few people saved these "common" coins when they were issued, and clad quarters often have weakly struck areas. Will they soar in price when collectors realize how scarce fully-struck, gem quality specimens may be? That's a prediction for the "Time Will Tell" file. (There already is one major book about post-1964 coins, *The United States Clad Coinage*, by Ginger Rapsus.)

Several survey respondents suggested buying or putting together piece-by-piece gem quality sets or partial sets of Washington quarters. The director of ANACS, Leonard Albrecht, listed Washington quarters of 1941 to 1964 in MS-66 grade or higher. Standing Liberty quarter specialist J.H. Cline of Palm Harbor, Florida, likes early mintmarked Washington quarters.

One collector suggested a short set of Washington quarters, 1932 to 1939, in MS-63 or higher grade. Georgia collector Bill Fivaz, who has two of the sharpest eyes in all of numismatics when it comes to locating rare die varieties, believes that "selective buying of eye appeal (toned or not) MS-65 specimens is almost a guaranteed excellent investment." But he also warns that at the present price levels, gem quality Washington quarters (along with Roosevelt dimes and fully-struck Jefferson nickels) "are highway robbery!"

According to many of the survey participants, Washington quarters are worthy of consideration. They're historic, have a nice design, and when wisely purchased, have a potential for increasing in value. Certainly, they're more than just two-bit coins.

Obverse

Reverse

Typical obverse and reverse of Connecticut copper pieces of 1785 to 1788, a popular Colonial coinage series. *(Photos by James A. Simek)*

CHAPTER EIGHTEEN

Colonial Copper Coins

"Impossible to find; getting expensive."

- Peter Boisvert -

When a $375 coin sells for $900, it is probably because: A) The buyer knew something about the coin the seller did not; B) The Chicago Cubs finally have won the World Series; therefore, the world has gone crazy; or C) None of the above.

Actually, that's a trick question, but a good introduction to U.S. Colonial coins, coins struck in or for use in the United States before the U.S. became the U.S. and before the Mint opened for business in Philadelphia. The particular coin referred to in the question above is a "Baby's Head" variety copper piece struck by the authority of the state of Vermont in 1786. It caught my attention in 1984 when a fine condition example of the colonial coin sold for $900, considerably more than its $375 "price guide" value at the time.

It emphasized again that while rare coin investors and speculators may hotly pursue attractive, historic coins that are available by the roll or by the bag, many collectors will pay higher than expected prices for genuinely scarce coins that usually don't even appear in "cuff-link quantity," two at a time. For example, if you wanted to purchase an entire bag—1,000 coins—of average uncirculated Morgan dollars it would take only a few telephone calls to obtain them. That's why U.S. silver dollars are so popular, there are enough pieces around to both promote them in the marketplace and fill most of the orders that come in.

A few specialized fields of U.S. numismatics such as Colonials are not covered regularly or at all by the major weekly and monthly value guides including *The Coin Dealer Newsletter* (popularly called the "Greysheet" because it's printed on grey paper). There just are not enough transactions on these coins. Yet, when significant specimens or quantities do enter the marketplace, the transactions indicate the strength of the collector market. That's what happened in the case of the $375 Vermont coin that sold at auction for $900.

Flip open a copy of the *Red Book* to the front section under Colonial coins. In the listing of state coinages you'll find Vermont. That New England state and four other nearby neighbors issued their own coinage following the events of July 4, 1776, because there was a need for making pocket change, and the U.S. Mint would not open until 1792. Among the Vermont listings and photographs is an interesting looking item struck in 1786 with what appears to be the head of a baby on the obverse. That's why this particular variety is called the Baby's Head. It's a major variety in a Colonial copper series that continues to attract the attention of collectors no matter what price guides might indicate. In the 1983 editions of the *Red Book*, Vermont Baby Head variety copper pieces were listed at $700 in fine condition, but market conditions seemed to indicate a downward trend because in 1984 they were listed at $500 in the same grade. By late summer, other value guides, such as *Coin Prices* magazine, indicated the coin's retail value at $375. Then along comes Mid-American Rare Coin Auction Company of Lexington, Kentucky, offering a sale with forty quality grade Vermont pieces, and determined buyers toss away the price guides. Despite price guide values ranging from $375 to $500, a Baby Head sold for an adult price of $900.

If you still have that copy of the *Red Book* handy, glance at the other Colonial coinage pages. In addition to Vermont, you'll see that Connecticut, Maryland, Massachusetts, New Hampshire, New York, New Jersey, and Vermont either authorized their own coinage, or someone in that state produced coins during the colonial period. Tokens and medals also were produced in other states during that era.

Colonial coins are eagerly collected by some numismatists even though you usually will not find these intriguing coins touted in weekly and monthly rare coin price guides and newsletters, and they are rarely the primary topic of the day in the dealer-to-dealer computer networks. In fact, unlike the superb gem quality specimens usually discussed on these dealer circuits, you'll find Colonial coins generally crudely struck, sometimes mis-struck, often on defective planchets, and more often than not with more than a hint of dirt, corrosion, and verdigris—a fancy name for rust.

With the exception of infrequent events such as the fabulous Johns Hopkins University Garrett Collection sales (conducted between 1979 and 1981), most Colonial coins usually are not available in About Uncirculated condition, let alone true Mint State. Sometimes the best-known examples of a rare variety may grade only Fine or Very Fine. U.S. Colonial coins definitely are not traded by the gem BU roll.

So, why are some collectors attracted to these peculiar coins? First, they represent a crucial period of early American history, when the young republic was struggling to survive. Second, this is one of the few areas of numismatics where you can purchase for less than $100 or $200 a coin struck in the United States that is so scarce there are less than a hundred specimens known.

A serious collector, armed with the knowledge available through the study of various early American copper research efforts, need only master a successful "poker face" to outwit virtually anyone whose numismatic scholarship is limited to a quick glance at the *Greysheet* and reliance on the annual *Red Book*. As collectors of the many varieties of U.S. half cents and large cents already know, when it comes to early American coppers, sole reliance on a grey sheet and a red book can leave you financially black and blue!

My personal collecting specialty is Connecticut copper pieces; historic, interesting coins struck by various parties from 1785 to 1788 both with and without the approval of the State of Connecticut to ease a severe shortage of coins for commerce prior to the opening of the U.S. Mint in Philadelphia. In the span of only four years, more than 400 varieties of Connecticut coppers were produced at several different sites, inside and outside that state. The *Red Book* devotes nearly four illustrated pages to the series, but lists only about three dozen varieties.

At a Sunday rare coin show with about two dozen dealers set up in a meeting room at the local YMCA, I once casually sorted through one dealer's "junk box" of foreign coins, searching for silver coins that might contain a higher bullion (intrinsic) value than the dealer's modest asking price. I was trying to cherrypick a winner and make a profit of a few percentage points for my efforts.

This particular dealer was no stranger to these monthly bourse events. He had three junk boxes on the table with three corresponding prices of 25 cents, 50 cents, and $1 per coin depending on the particular box from which the treasure emerged. As I began to poke in the sparsely populated $1 box, a copper coin immediately caught my attention. It was a 1787 Connecticut in very good condition, maybe even a shade better.

"How much?" I asked with the best straight face I could summon.

"It says $1 on the box, doesn't it?" the busy dealer almost snapped back.

I gave the dealer a $1 bill, nodded a "Thank you," and scurried to the corner of the large meeting room for a closer examination of my prize. It was not a true bell ringer, just a common date, common variety Connecticut, but in very good condition it should have sold at the time for about $25. I had just cherrypicked $24 in savings in addition to obtaining a needed coin for my collection. That coin now has a retail value of about $55. So, why was a "United States" coin that was pictured in the *Red Book* and worth at the time at least $25 floundering in a small sea of $1-a-piece coins of the world? I have a theory.

The legends on all Connecticut copper pieces are in Latin, not English. The coins apparently were intended to resemble British coins circulating in the colonies. If the junk box dealer did not read Latin or was unfamiliar with the legend's abbreviations AUCTORI CONNEC (by the authority of Connecticut) and INDE ET LIB (independence and liberty), he may have incorrectly believed this was a "foreign" coin. Also, since it was dated 1787 he may have felt it was worth a bit more than other coppers because it was so old; so into the $1 junk box it went. For how long it remained there I don't know. I do know it still reposes in my personal collection.

Survey participants recommended a wide range of Colonial coins including state-authorized issues and early attempts at federal coinage such as Nova Constellatio and Fugio coppers. The Nova coppers apparently were struck in England in 1785 at the request of Gouverneur Morris, a financial official of the young United States government. Morris proposed a decimal coinage system (as opposed to the cumbersome British system of coinage that circulated in the colonies). The Nova copper pieces are available in prices ranging from about $100 in Very Good to $800 to $1,000 in Extremely Fine, but silver pattern specimens are quite rare and cost more than many houses. Nova Constellatio copper pieces are considered tokens, rather than actual coins. There also are other "Nova" items, contemporary counterfeit pieces resembling British halfpence coins struck in New York state dated 1787 and with the legend "Nova Eborac."

Fugio cents actually are the first coins authorized by the United States government in 1787, but they were not struck in Philadelphia because the Mint did not begin making coins until 1792. Their major design feature is a sundial and the word "FUGIO," a reference to the Latin phrase, *tempus fugit*, "time flies." Depending on the variety, these coins can be obtained for about $150 to $1,000 in Very Good to Extremely Fine grades. Fugio cents are another example of history you can hold in your hand: the copper used to make these items reportedly came from the copper bands holding together powder kegs sent by the French to the Continental Army at the time of the Revolutionary War.

The motto on Fugio cents, "MIND YOUR BUSINESS," is attributed to Benjamin Franklin. Rare coin buyers and sellers are well advised to follow his recommendation.

Here are some comments about early American coins suggested by many survey respondents. Mark Borckardt, senior numismatist at Bowers and Merena Galleries of Wolfeboro, New Hampshire, stated: "For numismatic and historical importance, my personal recommendation involves United States Colonial coinage" (and also the early Large Cents from the Dr. Sheldon series; see chapter 12). Don Valenziano, Jr., of Hicksville, New York, suggested Fugio cents in XF-AU and major types of the Connecticut, New Jersey and Vermont copper coins in VF grade. New Jersey dealer Andy Lustig likes state coinage, Fugio and Nova coppers as well as Colonial era paper money. Some of these currency specimens were signed by the same dignitaries who signed the Declaration of Independence and other historically important documents.

Red Book editor Ken Bressett placed a 1652 Pine Tree shilling in VF condition high on his list. This coin, in that grade, probably will cost $3,000 or more, but it represents some of the first coinage of the settlers in the New World; indeed, some of the first coinage of North America! This silver coin is part of a series struck in Massachusetts depicting willow, oak, and pine trees, so the coins are known by their denomination and tree design—Pine Tree shilling, Oak Tree twopence, and so on.

Obverse   Reverse

Obverse   Reverse

Two vastly different types of Colonial coinage from Massachusetts: A silver Pine Tree shilling dated 1652 and a 1787 copper cent. *(Photos from James A. Simek)*

Other recommendations simply indicated purchasing high-grade Colonial coins, generally XF-AU condition. Milford, Massachusetts dealer Peter Boisvert likes high-grade Colonials, but warns they are "impossible to find; getting expensive." One collector suggested purchasing a few Colonial copper pieces in the $15 to $75 price range.

You can find many coins by bag quantities, but many Colonial coins are not available even by the roll.

Buyers and sellers of rolls and bags of coins may provide the numismatic marketplace with sparkle and sizzle, but collector coins continue to be the heartbeat that keeps the hobby alive. Colonial coins are close to the hearts of many of those collectors.

Obverse	Reverse
Obverse	Reverse
Obverse	Reverse

Among the coins in the Runners-Up category are the Liberty Head $20 gold pieces (1849 to 1907), two cent denomination copper coins (1864 to 1873), and the short-lived 20 cent silver pieces (1875 to 1878). *(Photos by James A. Simek)*

CHAPTER NINETEEN

Honorable Mentions

"All short-lived series."

- Gary Adkins -

The survey's runners-up for greatest number of recommendations were Hard Times and Civil War tokens, Liberty Head Double Eagles, two cent pieces and twenty cent pieces. An interesting mix of privately-issued items, and gold, silver and copper coins.

Hard Times and Civil War tokens fall under the category of "exonumia," a word that generally refers to numismatic items other than coins or paper money. Hard Times tokens were privately produced and distributed during—what else?—hard times, generally the period of 1833 to 1844. There was great controversy over the Bank of the United States, the availability of "hard" currency (copper, silver and gold coins), and the presidential administrations of Andrew Jackson and Martin Van Buren. Some political tokens issued during this period depict Jackson and Van Buren, some were designed to look like large cents, some carried advertising for the merchants who produced the tokens, and all of them capture an uneasy financial time in American history.

Civil War tokens, as their name implies, were issued during the "War Between the States," and served as a medium of exchange when legal tender copper coins started vanishing from circulation in the early 1860s. These tokens usually are divided between "patriotics" (those with patriotic slogans and designs) and "store cards" (those carrying advertising for the merchants who issued them). There are thousands of different varieties of Hard Times and Civil War tokens, and prices range from a few dollars each to tens of thousands of dollars.

Don Valenziano, Jr., sugested buying Hard Times tokens in Uncirculated grade. Illinois collector Bill Whisler put Civil War tokens (including patriotics and store cards) at the top of his listing. Silver Spring, Maryland, dealer Julian Leidman recommended tokens prior to the Civil War in XF or better. American Numismatic Association President and coin shop owner Kenneth L. Hallenbeck of Colorado Springs, Colorado, suggested "AU and Unc. Civil War and Hard Times tokens."

Liberty Head Double Eagles are the $20 gold pieces struck from 1849 to 1907, and there are several major types: Those without the IN GOD WE TRUST motto (1849 to 1866); those with the motto and denomination written as TWENTY D. (1866 to 1876); and Liberty Head $20 gold coins with the motto and the denomination shown as TWENTY DOLLARS (1877 to 1907). These later coins in VF-XF condition often can be purchased close to their bullion value. Of course, scarce dates such as those struck at the Carson City Mint cost much more, and high quality Mint State coins of any date usually command a significant premium. Proof "Libs" often have mintages of less than 100 coins each year. The proofs do not sell for melt value, unless you're referring to melting $20,000 or more worth of bullion to pay for one.

Two cent pieces were struck during the Civil War and are the first regular issue U.S. coins to carry the familiar motto, IN GOD WE TRUST. A little smaller in diameter than a twenty-five cent piece, these coins were struck from 1864 to 1873 with decreasing mintages each year and proof only specimens in 1873. Not exactly a beautiful coin when compared to the works of Saint-Gaudens, Weinman and other designers, the short-lived two cent piece certainly is an example of a coin that captures a moment in history; an end of the Civil War and a time when many in America prayed for unity and for the fathers, brothers and sons who died in the war.

Two survey respondents recommended red colored two cent pieces in MS-65 or better, while Orlando, Florida, dealer Jim Beasley of Tilden Coin Company says even scarcer date, lower mintage two cent pieces in XF/AU grade are less expensive coins that capture numismatic and historical importance, have beauty, and potential for increasing in value.

The Susan B. Anthony dollar of 1979 to 1981 was not the first U.S. coin to be utterly rejected by the public. The twenty cent denomination silver coins of 1875 to 1878 are included in that category. Just as Americans complained that "Susan B. Agony" coins looked too much like quarter dollars, so, too, did citizens of the 1870s regarding the twenty cent pieces. Numismatic history apparently repeats itself about every century.

Dean Schmidt of Kansas recommended purchasing a twenty cent piece in MS-65 grade or better. Winchester, Indiana, dealer Leon Hendrickson suggested MS-62 grade for a twenty cent piece.

Burnsville, Minnesota, dealer Gary Adkins listed "all short-lived series such as Flying Eagle cents [1856 to 1858], two cent, three cent, twenty cent pieces, etc."

If you're collecting short-lived U.S. coinage series you probably should include at least one specimen of the Susan B. Anthony dollar. Don't worry about not being able to locate one. Burnett Anderson, the Washington bureau correspondent for Krause Publications, reports there still are about a half-billion of them buried in government vaults. He estimates that at the current rate of dispersal there is a 500 year supply of these coins.

CHAPTER TWENTY

Consumer Protection

"If you cannot confirm the reliability of

the dealer, consider investing with

another firm."

-FTC/ANA pamphlet-

With the exception of policies imposed on advertisers by hobby publishers, local consumer fraud laws, and the U.S. Postal Service's rules, there are no nationwide regulations per se on the buying and selling of coins, except for Securities and Exchange Commission (SEC) regulations covering brokerage houses that have entered the market. That may change. The Federal Trade Commission (FTC) has been aggressively investigating the numismatic marketplace and by late 1990 there were indications the agency might recommend regulations or that Congress might pass specific legislation covering the buying and selling of rare coins.

A few numismatic industry groups have attempted self-regulation with varying degrees of success. Among the prominent efforts are those by American Numismatic Association (ANA), the Industry Council for Tangible Assets (ICTA), and the Professional Numismatists Guild (PNG). However, if there are enough abuses in the marketplace, various governmental agencies may get involved and impose mandatory requirements on buyers and sellers.

At an ICTA-sponsored seminar in Washington, D.C., in May 1990, Barry J. Cutler of the Federal Trade Commission's Consumer Protection Division warned the audience: "Unless the (numismatic) industry takes action to regulate itself fully through the Coin and Bullion Dealer Accreditation Program (CABDAP) or another organization, it will find itself regulated by the Federal Trade Commission, the Commodity Futures Trading Commission, or the Securities and Exchange Commission on unfavorable terms."

Louisiana Congressman James A. Hayes, a friend of the numismatic industry, agreed with Cutler's warnings: ". . . the [numismatic industry's] absence of action [could lead to] the worst possible form of federal regulation . . . you're suddenly going to have a federal agency as your partner that you didn't ask for. . . . [Without an effective industry self-regulation program, a federal agency could impose its own brand of regulation, and then Congress would have] a difficult time helping you and undoing the knots that are tied around you."

In the meantime, collectors and investors have a big task to become educated and responsible consumers. The following pages can be a big help.

The FTC and the ANA have produced a *Consumer Alert* brochure about investing in rare coins. The ANA is a nonprofit organization dedicated to numismatic education. Based in Colorado, it has about 32,000 members in the U.S. and other countries, and offers many educational programs for beginning and advanced collectors of coins, currency, tokens, and medals.

Since it was jointly issued by the FTC and the ANA in the summer of 1988, more than 100,000 copies of the brochure have been distributed. Here is the *Consumer Alert:*

Investing in Rare Coins

Buying rare coins can be a good investment and a satisfying hobby. But recently, for many Americans, it has become a financial disaster. Rare coin scams have increased and many Americans have lost most of their investment as a result of fraudulent sales practices. If you are investing in coins, the Federal Trade Commission and the American Numismatic Association urge you to protect yourself.

How to Protect Yourself

If you intend to buy rare or bullion coins for investment, your best protection is to spend time learning about the coins you are being asked to buy. In the past, most investment gains have gone to collectors, often known as numismatists, who have taken the time to study carefully various aspects of coins including rarity, grading, market availability, and price trends. Investment success over the years is the result of prudently acquiring coins of selected quality, proven rarity, and established numismatic desirability. Many careful buyers study coins for some time before buying even a single coin. Success can also be enhanced by researching dealers, as well as coins.

If you receive any solicitation about investing in coins, keep these points in mind.

Use common sense when evaluating any investment claims and do not rush into buying. Remember, anything that sounds too good to be true usually is not true.

Make sure that you know your dealer's reputation and reliability before you send money or authorize a credit card transaction. If you can, find out how long the company has been in business. Don't rely just on what a dealer's representative tells you on the phone. For example, if the dealer claims to be a member of a professional organization, call the organization and make sure that the claim is true. If you cannot confirm the reliability of the dealer, consider investing with another firm.

Do not be taken in by promises that the dealer will buy back your coins or that grading is guaranteed unless you are confident that the dealer has the financial resources to stand behind those promises. Many of the rare coin sellers prosecuted by the Federal Trade Commission during the last several years have not been able to meet guarantees and other obligations to their customers.

It is wise to get a second opinion from another source about the grade and value as soon as you receive your coins. So, before you buy, find out what remedies you will have if the second opinion differs. For example, some companies offer a 30-day return period if you are not satisfied with your purchase. Check the information that you are given. Will the full purchase price be refunded or will you be given a credit to be used for the purchase of other coins? If a dealer promises to buy back the coins at the same grade at which they were sold, does that mean at the price you paid or at some discounted price?

Be cautious about grading certificates, especially those furnished by coin dealers. Have the grades of any coins you buy checked by an independent source. If you use a grading certificate as a second opinion, be sure you understand what the certificate represents. Grading is not an exact science, and a certificate represents no more than the opinion of the certification service. Find out if the certification service is indeed independent of the dealer, and what grading standards are used. Also, because grading standards vary, coins certified by different services will be worth more or less than other coins of the same grade. Various periodicals list prices for coins. Check the prices for those coins you are considering.

Comparison shop. You need to be concerned not only with the grades, but with the prices as well. Visit several dealers before buying. Check prices in leading coin publications to make sure you are not being overcharged. Several publications list representative values for coins of various issues and grades. These values are higher than the prices consumers can expect to receive if they were to immediately sell their coins, and lower than the retail prices consumers may be charged to buy coins. Consult such publications prior to trusting dealers' representatives about the current value of coins. If a dealer's advertised price is much lower than the price listed in these publications, then the dealer may be misrepresenting the quality or grade of the coin.

Take possession of any coins you purchase to ensure they exist and to be sure that they are properly stored.

As with any consumer purchase, be wary about giving your credit card number to strangers, especially over the telephone.

How to Identify Fraudulent Sellers

The fact is: It is very difficult to identify fraudulent sellers of coins because they often look like legitimate dealers. For example, fraudulent sellers frequently produce attractive brochures or advertisements. They may claim to be the largest or finest dealers in the business. Because fraudulent sellers often appear to be reputable, it is particularly important to check the information that you are given.

Also, fraudulent sellers of coins often use many of the same techniques as legitimate dealers to attract buyers. Some advertise in newspapers and magazines. Others use a popular sales method known as telemarketing. For example, you may be approached about coin investing through an unsolicited telephone call, or you may be called after you have responded by mail to a print advertisement. Because telemarketing has grown so rapidly over the last several years, you should be particularly careful about committing yourself to any purchase from an unsolicited caller. Listed below are some sales techniques commonly used by dishonest dealers.

False Grading Claims

Usually, the value of a coin is determined by its grade and rarity, so it is very important that the coins you buy are graded correctly. The grade of a coin is a shorthand method of describing its condition. Because grading includes such factors as "overall appearance" and "eye appeal," it necessarily involves some degree of subjectivity. As a result, the grade assigned to a particular coin may vary even among legitimate dealers, especially in the higher, investment quality grades where distinctions in condition are more subtle. Because the fine distinctions between grades often mean large differences in the value or price of a coin, the subjectivity in grading means that there is some inherent risk in coin investing. Fraudulent sellers, however, often intentionally inflate the grades of the coins they sell, charging prices many times the coin's actual value. For example, you might pay $450 for an 1882-S Morgan Dollar, which was described to you as having a high grade because of its excellent condition. Later, however, you may find the accurate grade for the coin is two or more grades lower, and that coin is actually worth only $50. False grading is the most common form of rare coin fraud.

False Certification Claims

Many consumers and financial planners use certification services to verify grade before they buy. These services examine coins, "certify" them as to grade, and usually issue some form of grading certificate. However, consumers can lose money even when a certification service is used. Certification services provided by dishonest coin dealers are often part of fraudulent sales schemes and are intended to mislead consumers. In some instances, even certificates from legitimate services can be misleading. For example, some certification services use looser standards than those generally accepted by dealers in the coin market. As a result, the coins they certify may be worth less than other coins of the same grade. Before you buy any certified coin, make sure you check its current value. In addition, because grading standards have become more stringent over the years, a coin graded and certified in prior years may be given a lower grade today. Some fraudulent sellers may use an old certificate to mislead you into believing that a coin's grade is accurate. Be sure to check the date of any certificate you are offered and investigate the certification service before you commit to a purchase.

False Appreciation Claims

Dishonest dealers often mislead buyers by quoting appreciation rates for rare coins. What coins actually are being used for the index? Are they the same ones being offered to you? Remember, there is no guarantee that any coin will appreciate in value. Choose your dealer carefully.

Where to Go for Help

If you have a problem with a coin dealer or the dealer has not resolved the problem to your satisfaction, there are a number of places you can go for help. Some dealers will resolve disputes through binding arbitration by an independent third party, usually through one of their professional organizations. Consumer protection agencies, including the Federal Trade Commission, are interested in getting your complaint information to build cases against fraudulent dealers. Although most government offices are not able to resolve individual disputes, they can usually give you sound advice about how to proceed. The following list of organizations and government agencies is provided for your information.

Coin Organizations

The American Numismatic Association (ANA) is a nonprofit organization of coin collectors, but many dealers are also members. The ANA provides many educational programs for both novice and experienced collectors. If you have a complaint about an ANA member, you may write to the Association at 818 North Cascade Avenue, Colorado Springs, Colorado 80903. (There also is a toll-free telephone number for membership information, 800–367–9723.)

The Industry Council for Tangible Assets (ICTA) is a trade association for rare coin and bullion delaers. ICTA recently has begun a program to certify rare coin dealers who meet specified requirements, such as compliance with a code of conduct and submission of unresolved consumer complaints to binding arbitration. If you have a complaint about an ICTA dealer you may write to ICTA at 25 "E" Street, N.W., Washington, D.C. 20077.

The Professional Numismatists Guild (PNG) is an organization of coin dealers and numismatists. Membership in PNG is selective; to qualify a dealer must have a minimum number of years of experience and meet a minimum net worth requirement. The PNG also requires its members to submit to binding arbitration to resolve complaints filed by consumers or other dealers. If you have a complaint against a PNG member, you may write to the PNG at P.O. Box 430, Van Nuys, California 91408.

Other Agencies

The Better Business Bureau is interested in the business practices of companies in your area. Contact the BBB in the city where the coin dealer is located.

The State Consumer Protection Agency or Attorney General's office may be interested in your complaint information. Contact the state consumer protection agency or the Attorney General's office in the state where the coin dealer is located.

The U.S. Postal Inspector should be contacted if you have a complaint and you ordered, received or paid for your coins through the mail. Postal inspectors are listed under "Postal Service" in the U.S. Government section of your local phone book.

The Federal Trade Commission is interested in receiving your complaint information. Write to Federal Trade Commission, 6th & Pennsylvania, N.W., Washington, D.C. 20580.

CHAPTER TWENTY-ONE

Buying Coins

"Is that the best you can do?"

- frequent buyer's and seller's lament -

Shopping for rare coins is easy. You can simply grab the latest issue of your favorite hobby publication and browse through the many diverse, colorful advertisements while comfortably sitting in your favorite chair, lazily lounging in bed, or sunbathing on a park bench. But frequently, collectors are seized by an overpowering urge to personally attend a rare coin show where dozens, sometimes hundreds of live, walking-talking dealers may confront and even confound them.

Whether you've never attended a show, or you're a seasoned veteran of such mega-events as the annual American Numismatic Association (ANA) convention held each summer or the Florida United Numismatists (FUN) convention each January, here are tips of the trade for an enjoyable visit and effective coin buying.

First, a definition. For some reason, Americans use a French word to refer to the area of a coin show where the buying and selling is supposed to take place, the *bourse*. Sometimes you'll see buyers and sellers huddled in the outside corridors and hallways near vending machines or elsewhere, but the designated location for official transactions is the floor of the bourse.

Funk & Wagnalls New International Dictionary of the English Language defines the word as "An exchange or money market. . . ." It also points out the word originally meant a purse or bag. Perhaps that's appropriate. The prices of some coins require a deep purse to buy them.

Anyway, the main buying and selling action at a coin show is on the bourse floor. Buyers who grossly paid too much for an item may be found sprawled on the bourse floor, but that's another story.

To locate the nearest coin show, scan the sometimes lengthy calendar listings in various numismatic publications. The shows are usually listed by both date of the individual event and region of the country where it will be held. These notices often include information about the number of dealers who may be setting up tables, whether there will be an admission fee, and where to obtain more information about the show.

Unless you live in a remote part of the country, chances are good there will be a coin show within an hour's drive at least once or twice a year, if not more frequently. In major urban areas, there usually are several nearby coin shows every month, if not each weekend. Plenty of ways to spend your time and money close to home.

Coin shows range in size from a half dozen, part-time neighborhood dealers gathered at the cozy, local Holiday Inn or Moose Lodge to huge regional and national conventions of organized numismatic organizations, shows that attract hundreds of prominent dealers from around the world and thousands of other participants. No matter how big or small the show may be, there are basic rules you should follow.

1. Be prepared. Just like the famous Boy Scouts motto, be prepared to have an enjoyable visit at the coin show by arming yourself with knowledge.

Make sure you know the exact location of the coin show and the hours the bourse will be open to the public. Usually, the dealers have an hour to themselves on the bourse floor each morning of the show before the doors open to the public, and sometimes if business is slow they'll pack up and leave their tables an hour or two before the show is scheduled to close for the day.

It's frustrating for a collector to arrive at a show a full hour before its scheduled closing time and find nearly all the dealers' tables deserted. But it happens.

Before you even enter the bourse area you may be required to register. Even if there is no admission charge, some coin shows issue "credentials" to visitors, some sort of name tag or badge that may be required to enter the room where the dealers have set up their tables and display cases filled with numismatic goodies.

Prominently wear the tag or badge when you enter the room and while you are there, but promptly remove it when you leave. Wearing it outside the bourse could become unsolicited advertising to lure potential thieves who might be lurking near the show, waiting to rob an unsuspecting coin collector or dealer. Of course, never leave valuables unattended, out of sight, or out of mind.

If you're going to a big show, wear comfortable shoes. You may do a lot of walking, probably on a concrete floor, so dress neatly and comfortably. You'll notice some dealers dress for success by wearing three-piece, pin-striped business suits and silk ties. Others appear as though they've been sitting through a hot July double-header at Shea Stadium. That's just the nature of the industry. What really counts is what the dealer offers customers in the way of experience, knowledge, integrity and, of course, merchandise.

However, if even the young children sitting behind a dealer's table are wearing diamond pinky rings and Rolex wristwatches, the clothing may be a clue the profit margins there could be slightly higher than the entire gross national product of Peru.

Larger coin shows provide visitors with printed programs listing the participating dealers and their display table numbers to make it easy to find out who is where on the bourse floor. Sometimes the program also provides a listing of dealers by the type(s) of material they sell, for example silver dollars, currency, or numismatic books. You can scan the program, make notes about which dealers you'll visit, and begin your journey with specific destinations. Or, you can just begin at one end of the room and work your way up and down each aisle while looking into every dealer's display cases until you spot something that deserves closer attention.

That last method of "window shopping" may require a full day or even several days at the larger coin conventions where 400 or more dealers may be represented at the show. Even after only a few hours of browsing you may believe that despite the definition of Funk & Wagnalls, *bourse* is the French word for swollen feet.

2. Know what you really are looking to purchase and approximately how much you really want to pay. This involves the compilation of a "want list," as in the phrase, "I want to buy a 1921 Morgan dollar in Very Good condition." Sometimes your notes are more accurately described as a "wish list," as in the phrase, "Boy, I wish I could afford to buy an 1804 dollar in ANY condition."

There generally are two ways to make a want list. One common way is to divide the list into categories, such as Lincoln cents, silver three cent pieces, and Liberty Head gold eagles, and under each category write down the specific coins you want, along with a note about the grade you desire and a retail price range you'd be willing to pay for the item(s).

The second want list method is for compulsive buyers. Forget writing up a list, just carry a copy of *A Guide Book of United States Coins* (the "Red Book") and start purchasing one of everything. At international coin shows, bring a shopping cart to lug the telephone book-sized *Standard Catalog of World*

Coins. Also, obtain a bumper sticker that reads *SHOP TILL YOU DROP* and wear it across your back.

At the show you may see collectors of all ages with bulging back pockets. The bulges are caused by massive quantities of price guides; folded, well-read copies of *The Coin Dealer Newsletter* (the famous "Greysheet"), the price guide sections of *Coin World* and *Numismatic News, Coin Prices Magazine,* and other literature that will help a potential buyer determine the current value of various numismatic items.

Remember, these items are only price GUIDES. As yet, no Guru of Grading or Sultan of Slabs has been able to produce a price guide that is 100 percent accurate for every single coin at every particular moment in time. Because of changes in the marketplace, coins offered for sale often are legitimately priced significantly higher or lower than even the most recently printed guide.

3. Bring a magnifying glass. Experts may disagree on the specific magnification power that is best, but generally a good quality three to five power glass will help detect value-dropping imperfections or uncover value-adding varieties on most coins. For closer examinations of mint errors like die doubling or re-punched mintmarks, ten to twenty power magnification may be helpful.

At the 1988 ANA convention in Cincinnati, a 100 power microscope would have been useful to find the alleged hot dogs in the buns being sold at the bourse floor concession stand. But again, that's another story.

4. If there are educational seminars or coin club meetings being conducted in conjunction with the show, take time to attend one or more meetings. You not only may learn interesting information, you may fall in love with another fascinating area of numismatics. Don't be shy. Most collectors' clubs enjoy having non-members attend their meetings and will warmly welcome you to take part in their gatherings. Educational seminars and club meetings are an integral part of the annual conventions of the ANA, FUN, and many

regional numismatic groups such as the Central States Numismatic Society (CSNS). You'll learn more about the hobby and probably establish life-long friendships at these important gatherings.

Numismatics is more than just the current Bid and Ask quotations on a price guide. Belonging to a coin club is a wonderful way to discover the hobby.

5. Learn bourse floor etiquette. While strolling the aisles, eager to ask questions about specific items for sale, be patient. If a dealer obviously is in the middle of a major sale ("a deal"), you can either quietly go on to the next table or politely interrupt during a lull in the conversation to ask if you should return in a few minutes to inquire about certain coins. Most dealers will be happy to give you more than just the time of day.

Sure, now and then you may encounter a rude dude; if so, there are all those other dealers at the other tables in the room who will be delighted to serve your needs.

Although it may seem that most coins today are "slabbed," many are still "raw" (unslabbed, and easily removed from temporary holders). Whether slabbed or raw, handle the coins carefully—and do it close to the tabletop. Even if you're examining a corroded 1907 Indian cent in about good condition, hold it by the edges. And don't sneeze on it.

Most coin dealers will accept checks in payment, but will want to see your drivers license and perhaps a major credit card (Visa, MasterCard, American Express, etc.). Some dealers accept these credit cards for purchases, but may charge a fee to cover the costs charged to them by the card company.

6. Bargain in good faith. If the dealer quotes you a price that you believe is too much, don't lecture him about being able to buy it for less two aisles away. Ask if that is the best price he can offer. If you still are not satisfied with the asking price, return the coin and just simply say, "Thanks, but I'm going to look a bit more," or "Thanks, but I'll pass."

No two coins are exactly alike. If one dealer asks $15 for an 1874 dime in fine condition, and another wants $18 for "the same" coin, there may be solid reasons why there's a difference in price. First, are both coins actually in the same condition? No matter what the label on the holder claims, the actual coin may be in better or worse condition. Second, the dealer asking $15 may have had that coin in his inventory for months or years and wants to sell it rather than open a museum with it.

The dealer quoting $18 may have recently purchased the coin for, say $10 or $14, and is asking a fair price based on his own costs. So, don't be afraid to ask if the quoted price is the final offer.

When my son was about seven years old and wanted to purchase some inexpensive items at a coin show, I taught him to always ask, "Is that the best you can do?" I patiently waited a few feet away while a dealer added up my son's three items and declared the cost would be fifty cents.

"Is that the best you can do?" asked the boy.

"OK," the surprised dealer responded. "You can have it for *forty* cents."

At an early age, the youngster learned a valuable lesson —and saved 20 percent!

However, now at the age of seventeen, his attention unfortunately has turned from coins to cars, so when he's informed he can have the family car for only an hour, he asks, "Is that the best you can do?"

But, that's another story.

CHAPTER TWENTY-TWO

How Much Is It Worth?

"A sure-fire seven step guide to

determining the value of your

collection."

- Donn Pearlman (with tongue lodged firmly

in cheek) -

Coin collectors frequently ask themselves, "Gee, I wonder how much my collection is worth?" The average collector will ask this question about three or four times a day.

Pondering this often elusive question probably consumes more time each day than talking with family members at the dinner table. Unless, of course, other family members are collectors, too, in which case, the phrase, "Gee, I wonder how much my collection is worth?" is heard echoing through the household several times an hour.

Answering this apparently simple question actually can be a complicated matter. Factors such as the specific coins in your collection, their individual condition, current market demand for these items, your astrological (Zodiac) sign, the barometer reading and other atmospheric conditions all must be painstakingly considered. To speed up the process, here's a sure-fire, seven step guide to determining the value of your collection.

STEP 1: Locate each of the rare coins, currency items, tokens, medals, and other assorted numismatic specimens you've accumulated over the years. Allow yourself four to five weeks just to scour the drawers and closet in your bedroom. If you live in an apartment, figure another three weeks per room. If you live in a house, allow three weeks per room and another full month to check out the basement or utility room. Forget the attic entirely; you don't want to know what's up there.

STEP 2: Assemble in the same room all of the items you've discovered. In some cases this will require moving to a larger apartment or house. If you're serious about learning the true value of your collection, you'll do it.

STEP 3: Once all of your accumulated collectibles have been assembled in the same room, take a week's vacation at Club Med. You'll need to rest because the really hard work is still ahead.

STEP 4: Within three hours of your return from the Caribbean begin making a comprehensive listing of every item in your collection. Armed with enough paper to copy the entire Greater Los Angeles telephone directory, be sure to carefully examine and make accurate notes about each piece for the following vital information:

> A. Country of origin
> B. Denomination
> C. Date
> D. Mintmark
> E. Variety (such as Flowing Hair, Braided Hair, Thinning Hair, etc.)

F. Type (such as Large Letters, Small Letters, Scarlet Letters, etc.)

Here's a helpful tip: It's best to carefully sort the items as you catalogue them. Place all the pieces from one country in one room of your apartment or house, all items from other countries in other rooms. If you specialize in coins and currency of the United Nations you may have to temporarily rent the nearest Holiday Inn or Hyatt Hotel. If you really love your collection, you'll do it.

Within each country, sort the items by denomination, then by date, mintmark, and finally by variety and type. If you need more space, either get another place to live or just carefully place coins one on top of each other. However, if you collect decadrachms of ancient Syracuse or high relief U.S. 1907 Roman numeral $20 gold pieces, you're out of luck. They don't stack real well. So, you still may have to find larger quarters to continue sorting your dimes and dollars.

STEP 5: Now that you've classified each numismatic specimen using the above guidelines, it's time to determine the most crucial factor in their value, each item's true grade.

To properly accomplish this important task you'll need the following equipment:

A. 3 power magnifying glass
B. 10 power magnifying glass
C. 15 to 20 power magnifying glass
D. 100,000 power electron scanning microscope
E. Adequate lighting. Generally, only two types of lights are needed to carefully examine a coin's surface. Many hardware and light fixture stores sell small, table-top, high-intensity lamps, then check the Yellow Pages to obtain a 30,000 watt antiaircraft spotlight.

Using these easy to obtain optical and lighting accessories, again carefully examine each rare coin, piece of paper money, token and medal in your collection, but this time make notes about the following:

A. Nicks, scrapes, dents, or gouges that readily can be seen with the naked eye in semi-darkness from twenty feet away. These coins should be labeled, "MS-65 Prior to the 1982 Changes in the Industry's Grading Standards."

B. Surface blemishes that are prominently visible only when viewed using the 3X magnifying glass. Label these items, "Arm's Length Gem."

C. Small, but noticeable detracting contact marks that can be seen using the 10X magnifier. Label these, "Nice for Type."

D. The smallest of abrasions or hairline marks visible only when using the 15 to 20X magnification. Label these items, "Premium MS-65 Quality When I Bought It."

E. Absolutely no blemishes even when examined with the electron scanning microscope under illumination of the 30,000 watt spotlight, a flawless specimen with full mint luster and natural color. Label these, "Currently MS-64 Quality When I Try to Sell It."

STEP 6: Re-examine each coin to determine its current grade using all of the following grading guides and criteria:

A. American Numismatic Association Grading Standards for United States Coins

B. Photograde

C. Accu-Grade

D. Brown & Dunn

E. Green & Slimy

F. Black & Blue

G. Sports Illustated Famous Numismatists Swimsuit Edition

H. The Audubon Society Annual Report (see the section entitled "Is Coin Grading for the Birds?")

STEP 7: Match up your extensive notes with price guide listings found in various hobby publications, weekly and monthly price guides, and on the "Bid Board" at your neighborhood coin shop or your local coin club meeting.

Calculate the total value by adding together the average price guide listings of each individual item. Finally, to calculate the actual wholesale value of your entire collection, simply divide the total, aggregate amount by a number equal to the sum of your height, weight, and age.

Now you've finally answered the frequent, perplexing question, "Gee, I wonder how much my collection is worth?"

In a future book, we'll take a look at answering the question, "Where the heck am I going to store this antiaircraft spotlight?"

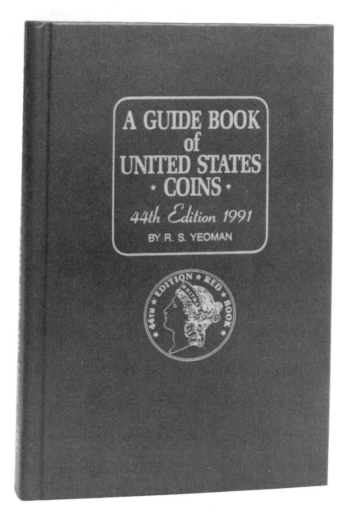

One of the most important items in almost everyone's coin collection, an up-to-date copy of the *Red Book*. *(Photo courtesy Western Publishing Co.)*

CHAPTER TWENTY-THREE

Where to Turn Now

"Buy the book before the coin."

- Aaron Feldman -

Now that your leg has just been firmly pulled by that last chapter, here are certainly more traditional methods for both determining the value of your coins and learning about them. One of the most frequently offered pieces of advice offered by veteran collectors to beginners is the statement attributed first to the late Ohio dealer Aaron Feldman, "Buy the book before the coin." Read about the subject first before making a rare coin or currency purchase.

One of the best ways to determine what you want to collect in United States coins is to sit down with a copy of one of the most important books in numismatics, *A Guide Book of United States Coins,* commonly called the *Red Book* because of its distinctive red cover. The *Red Book* has been around for more than four decades, first edited by the late R.S. Yeoman and now by Kenneth Bressett, and an updated version is produced annually. The more than 280 pages of the latest edition are filled with excellent quality photographs ranging from the earliest coins of North America to the most recent issues from the U.S. Mint. Capsule comments about the coins are presented along with listings of approximate retail values of coins in various grades.

The publisher of the *Red Book*, Western Publishing Company, Inc., Racine, Wisconsin, proudly proclaims the annual editions as "the most frequently used numismatic reference for details concerning all aspects of United States coins. Historical data, mintage records, coinage statistics and values are listed for all issues from the Colonial period starting in 1616 through the most recent varieties of this year's coinage." All this for only $8.95, and it is available at virtually all coin and hobby shops and many bookstores.

There also is a *Blue Book*, R.S. Yeoman's *Handbook of United States Coins*, also edited by Kenneth Bressett. This annual reference guide contains average prices dealers will pay for U.S. coins in various grades from About Good to MS-63. The suggested retail price for the *Blue Book* is $4.95. For more information about these books write to Western Publishing Company, Inc., Department M, P.O. Box 700, Racine, Wisconsin 53401.

The *Coin World Almanac*, sixth edition, is another handy reference guide with more than 500,000 facts about coins, collecting, and numismatics in general. Appropriately described by its publisher, Amos Press, as "a must for the numismatic bookshelf of every conscientious collector," this hardcover book has 744 pages and sells for $29.95 (softcover is $15.95).

Amos Press has also prouduced the *Comprehensive Catalog & Encyclopedia of United States Coins* including pre-federal coinage, pioneer gold coins, and pattern coinage. More than 800 photographs fill this important new addition to numismatic libraries. This 464 page book is available in both paperback ($19.95) and hardcover ($35.00) editions. Amos Press has a toll-free number for information and ordering of these and other books, 1-800-253-4555 (in Ohio, 1-513-498-0800).

Also highly recommended is any book by Q. David Bowers, but why not start with his latest, *A Buyer's Guide to the Rare Coin Market*, published in 1990 and priced at $9.95. In the past thirty years Bowers has produced almost as many books as the telephone company. In 1975 or so, an AU condition copy of his 1964 book, *Coins and Collectors* turned me into a reborn numismatist. That's still a very good book, but an even better one is Bowers' *Adventures With Rare Coins* ($24.95) or the more advanced *The History of United States Coinage* ($49.00). Information about his books can be obtained by writing to Bowers and Merena at the address listed below under the publication, *Rare Coin Review*.

The Investor's Guide to Coin Trading by Scott A. Travers, described by former *New York Times* coin columnist Ed Reiter as "quite possibly, the most significant book ever to focus on a collectible—any kind of collectible—as a vehicle for investment." 230 pages, hardcover, $24.95

Also by Travers, *Coin Collector's Survival Manual*, 218 pages, $12.95. Both can be ordered from Travers at 599 Lexington Ave., Suite 2300, New York, New York 10022. Telephone: 212-836-4787.

Travers covers the crucial subject of grading in his books, but a solid numismatic library needs one or more books specifically devoted to this subject. *A.N.A. Grading Standards for United States Coins* is the American Numismatic Association's guidelines. Line drawings accompany easy to follow narrative to help readers quickly match up their coins with the appropriate grades. First published in 1977, a revised, fourth edition of the book was produced for 1991. In 1990, Ivy Press, Inc., published *How to Grade U.S. Coins* by Dallas dealer and ANA Governor James L. Halperin. This is another easy to use, step by step guide that concentrates on mint state and proof coins. Black and white and color photographs provide a quick reference on where to first look on a coin's surfaces when determining the grade. The 167 page book is priced at $14.95 and available from Heritage Rare Coin Galleries, Dallas (see below under *Legacy* magazine).

For those interested in world coins, the place to start is the *Standard Catalog of World Coins*, by Chester L. Krause and Clifford Mishler. The 1991 edition has 1,920 pages with nearly 46,000 photos of legal tender coins from around the world struck since 1801. Mintage figures, precious metal weights, even historical background information are contained in the "telephone book" of world coins, $36.95.

Here are a few other books about world coinage and ancient numismatic items. This is just a small sampling of some of the current literature. The American Numismatic Association library has many, many more items, and the library is one of the wonderful reasons to become an ANA member. You can easily borrow books by mail.

Seaby's Standard Catalogue of British Coins, twenty-fifth edition, lists values for the English series from Celtic coinage to Elizabeth II, 351 pages, $22.00

Greek Imperial Coins and Their Values by David R. Sear lists 6,000 coins and their values and plenty of information with 1,750 illustrations and even 10 maps. 636 pages, hardcover, $80.00

Also by Sear, *Greek Coins and Their Values Volume I: Europe* lists nearly 4,000 coins and their values arranged in geographical order from Spain to Crete. Among the 1,500 illustrations are photographs of coins from the British Museum collection, 317 pages, hardcover, $50. And, *Greek Coins and Their Values Volume II: Asia & Africa* with about 4,500 coins listed with 2,000 photos of Hellenic coinage from the earlier electrum coins of Ionia and Lydia to kingdoms of the Hellenistic Age, 762 pages, hardcover, $50.00.

Roman Coins and Their Values, fourth edition, by David R. Sear covers coinage of the Roman Republic and Imperial Rome with more than 4,300 coins listed and 900 photographs, 400 pages, hardcover, $70.00.

If you haven't run out of bookshelf space yet, here are even more highly recommended books.

The Cherrypickers Guide to Rare Die Varieties by Bill Fivaz and J.T. Stanton shows over 160 varieties. At $14.95 the book probably pays for itself the first time you spot a scarce variety underpriced in a dealer's display case. The book contains excellent close-up photography.

The Early Paper Money of America by Eric P. Newman, third edition. A delightful 480 pages from Colonial era notes to 1800. This revised edition is $49.95 plus $2.50 shipping per book. Krause Publications, Catalog Department, 700 East State Street, Iola, Wisconsin 54990. 1-800-258-0929.

The Early Coins of America by Sylvester S. Crosby, originally published in 1875, it has been reprinted several times. This dull-reading, basic reference on U.S. Colonial coinage provides information about the political and legislative history as well as the types and varieties of state coinages. There are line drawings, but unfortunately, no photographs. Still, it provides a tremendous amount of information about Colonial era coinage.

United States Paper Money, ninth edition, by Chester L. Krause and Robert F. Lemke, edited by Bob Wilhite. The 1990 edition contains over 600 photographs of U.S. paper money from 1812 to the present with more than 14,000 price guide values. National Bank notes also include rarity ratings for each bank issue, $21.95. Krause Publications has a toll-free number to order these and other books, 1-800-258-0929 (in Wisconsin 1-715-445-2214).

Price Guides

There are about a dozen publications that regularly track coin and currency values on a weekly or monthly basis. Here are some of the best to consider.

The Coin Dealer Newsletter
P.O. Box 11099
Torrance, California 90510

Phone: 213-515-7369

Usually just referred to as the "Greysheet." A weekly newsletter that provides reliable, timely information on wholesale bid levels of frequently traded "raw" (unslabbed) U.S. coins. A monthly summary newsletter also provides additional information on coins by date and mintmark. Six month subscription (32 issues), $50; one year (63 issues), $89; two years (126 issues), $147.

The Certified Coin Dealer Newsletter
P.O. Box 11099
Torrance, California 90510

Phone: 213-515-7369

The so-called "Bluesheet" (because it's printed on blue paper) is the weekly equivalent of the *Greysheet* for slabbed (certified) coins. Six month subscription, $56; one year, $99; and two years, $164.

The Currency Dealer Newsletter
P.O. Box 11099
Torrance, California 90510

Phone: 213-515-7369

This monthly newsletter is printed on green paper and, therefore, is called the "Greensheet," but you probably could have guessed that by now. It tracks values of major types of U.S. paper money. One year subscription (12 issues), $35; two years (24 issues), $61.

Major Hobby Newspapers & Magazines

To keep up with new discoveries, current activities of collectors' groups, dealers, and for a wonderful source of advertisements offering to buy and sell numismatic merchandise, there are many fine weekly, bi-weekly and monthly publications. Consider these to start.

Bank Note Reporter
700 East State Street
Iola, Wisconsin 54990

Phone: 715-445-2214

The hobby's leading independent paper money publication provides readers with news and market data on U.S. notes, world notes, stock certificates, bonds, checks, scrip, and more. You can get a free one month trial subscription to this monthly newspaper. If you don't like the first issue, write "cancel" on the invoice and return it.

One year subscription (12 issues), $23.95; sample copy, $2.25.

COINage
2660 East Main Street
Ventura, California 93003

Phone: 805-643-3664

A large monthly publication produced by Miller Magazines, Inc., usually filled with color photographs and articles by some of today's best numismatic writers. The senior editor, Ed Reiter, is a former columnist for the *New York Times.* The editorial content usually is a mix of historical information, current and proposed coinage, and marketplace background and anaylsis. Available at many newsstands across the country at $2.50 per copy, *COINage* is also available by mail-order subscription. One year (12 issues), $18; two years, $30; three years, $42.

Coins
700 East State Street
Iola, Wisconsin 54990

Phone: 715-445-2214

Monthly magazine focusing on articles geared toward the beginning collector as well as veterans. Informative features, news updates, and a monthly value guide for U.S. coins. Available at many newsstands, hobby shops, and by mail at $18.50 for a one year (12 issues) subscription; sample copy, $2.50.

There is a companion publication, *Coin Prices*, that contains a comprehensive value listing of virtually every regular issue United States coin. Subscriptions are $15.95 per year; sample copy $2.95.

Coin World
911 Vandemark Road
Sidney, Ohio 45365

Phone: 513-498-0800

Billed as "the news weekly for the entire numismatic field," the thick, weekly issues live up to that promotional slogan. Sometimes leading crusades against suspected wrong-doing or pushing on behalf of certain numismatic-related causes, *Coin World* is read by more than 80,000 subscribers; beginners through advanced collectors, investors and dealers.

The newspaper's Trends section started a trend in price guides, giving readers a comprehensive listing of U.S. rare coin values, and regularly provides price guide information for coins of other countries, such as Canada. Trends editor Keith M. Zaner writes a short weekly column explaining marketplace activities.

Sold at many hobby stores and newsstands with a cover price of $1.95. One year subscription (52 issues), $26; two years (104 issues), $46.

Numismatic News
700 East State Street
Iola, Wisconsin 54990

Phone: 715-445-2214

Started on his kitchen table as a newsletter more than a quarter century ago by Chester Krause, *Numismatic News* has become the weekly flagship of a fleet of more than two dozen various hobby newspapers and magazines produced by Krause Publications. Current events, historical features, letters to the editor and guest columns fill each weekly edition. Each issue also includes a four page coin market report similar in format to the *Greysheet*, providing readers with a quick reference guide to the average wholesale and retail prices for commonly traded U.S. coinage. These weekly features also include a brief, insightful market analysis and commentary by editor Bob Wilhite. An expanded monthly price guide tracks a wide range of U.S. coins in various grades.

Available at many hobby shops and some newsstands at $1.25 per copy, subscriptions by mail are: Six months, $12.95; one year, $24.95; two years, $46.50; three years, $67.

World Coin News
700 East State Street
Iola, Wisconsin 54990

Phone: 715-445-2214

A newspaper produced every two weeks devoted exclusively to coins of the world, old and new. Senior editor Colin R. Bruce II is actively involved in the invaluable reference book, *The Standard Catalog of World Coins*. New Issues editor Fred Borgmann does an outstanding job keeping track of various interesting new coins from around the world, and regular columnists such as Harlan J. Berk (see chapter 10) make each issue a delight for collectors of everything from classical ancient coinage to the latest Isle of Man commemoratives. Subscriptions are $24.95 per year; sample copy, $1.50.

Dealers' Newsletters & Magazines

Several dealerships are producing high-quality newsletters and magazines that are worthy of your attention. Here are some of them.

Legacy
Heritage Plaza
Highland Park Village
Dallas, Texas 75205-2788

Phone: 800-872-6467 (in Texas, 214-528-3500)

A slick publication that at first glance appears as though it could easily hold its own on the rack at a newsstand. *Legacy* actually is a price list for Heritage Rare Coin Galleries of Dallas, although the magazine usually carries advertisements for competing dealerships. Sharp photographs, many in full color, outstanding articles and interviews all make this quarterly publication one of the finest in numismatics. Single copies are $5 each, annual subscriptions are $14.95. Call first, they sometimes will provide free copies for the asking.

Rare Coin Review
c/o Bowers and Merena
Box 1224
Wolfeboro, New Hampshire 03894-1224

Phone: 800-458-4646 (in New Hampshire, 603-569-5095)

As with *Legacy,* this glossy-paper publication of around 100 or so pages primarily serves as a price list. Bowers and Merena Galleries is also one of the largest numismatic dealerships in the United States. *Rare Coin Review* always contains eye-opening articles and commentary, and just reading the sometimes detailed descriptions of coins in the price list will give even casual buyers the beginnings of a solid numismatic education. Because of its well deserved reputation, early issues of this publication often appear in numismatic book sales and auctions. Single copies are $5 each, write for the latest subscription information about *Rare Coin Review* and the company's "grand format" auction catalogues.

The Reader's Edge
Hanks & Associates
415 North Mesa
El Paso, Texas 79901

Phone: 915-544-8188

A four page newsletter that quickly established itself as an accurate forecaster of numismatic marketplace trends. Hanks & Associates created "a rock to base decisions upon," two rare coin indexes similar to the stockmarket's Dow Jones Industrial Average. These are "The Reader's Edge 88" and the "Generic 30" rare coin averages. The "88" is based on 88 high quality rare coins, the "30" is composed of 30 of the most popular and widely traded coins and indicates prices a dealer, collector or investor could receive for the coins from Hanks & Associates. Copies of this highly informative newsletter are free, just write to the above address and request one.

The Rosen Numismatic Advisory
c/o Numismatic Counseling, Inc.
Box 38
Plainview, New York 11803

Dealer Maurice Rosen is well known in the industry for publishing revealing interviews with marketplace insiders. He also coined the phrase "Grading Renaissance" to explain the drastic changes in rare coin grading that occurred in the early to mid-1980s. One year subscription to the monthly newsletter is $79.

The Winning Edge
Ellesmere Numismatics
P.O. Box 915
Danbury, Connecticut 06813

Phone: 800-426-3343 (in Connecticut, 203-794-1232)

Another informative newsletter worthy of consideration that is produced by a dealership closely involved in the marketplace. The goal seems to be to arm coin buyers with crucial information about the marketplace so they can make informed decisions on what to buy and sell. Six month subscription usually is $24, however, call first as they often provide discounts, or even free copies.

Specialized Newsletters and Clubs

Some collectors' groups produce their own, excellent publications devoted to their particular specialty. These are some of the major groups and publications.

Barber Coin Collectors Society
P.O. Box 5353
Akron, Ohio 44313
   or
BCCS
P.O. Box 382246
Memphis, Tennessee 38138

Dues are $10 per year and include copies of the *Journal of the Barber Coin Collectors Society.*

Bust Half Nut Club
P.O. Box 4875
Margate, Florida 33063

An informal organization of collectors who are "nuts" about Bust type half dollars. Write for current information about dues and the newsletter.

The Celator
P.O. Box 123
Lodi, Wisconsin 53555

A small, but award-winning monthly newspaper that has evolved into a magazine devoted to classical ancient numismatics and antiquities. There are news items, book reviews, even puzzles, trivia questions, and a cartoon. Subscriptions are $24 per year.

The Colonial Newsletter
P.O. Box 4411
Huntsville, Alabama 35802

A scholarly publication that sometimes is issued twice a year, usually three times, and now and then even four times a year, depending on the number of manuscripts received and the current workload of the editor, J.C. Spilman. Write for current subscription rates.

Civil War Token Society
c/o Donna Morgan, Secretary
P.O. Box 330
Garnerville, New York 10923
    or
Civil War Token Society
P.O. Box 951988
Lake Mary, Florida 32795 - 1988

Dues are $7 and include a subscription to the quarterly publication *Civil War Token Journal*.

Early American Coppers
P.O. Box 15782
Cincinnati, Ohio 45215

Dues are $16 per year and include *Penny-Wise*, the EAC's scholarly, yet lively journal devoted primarily to large and half cents, but also with a smattering of colonial era copper.

International Bank Note Society
P.O. Box 1642
Racine, Wisconsin 53401

Write to the above address for current dues information.

John Reich Journal
David J. Davis, Editor
P.O. Box 205
Ypsilanti, Michigan 48197

Named after an early mint engraver, this publication covers U.S. gold and silver coins prior to the start of the

Seated Liberty design. Dues for the John Reich Society are only $10 per year and include the journal.

Liberty Seated Collectors Club
c/o John Kroon
P.O. Box 1062
Midland, Michigan 48641

Dues are $11 and include a subscription to *The Gobrecht Journal for Collectors of the Seated Liberty Coin Series.*

Society for U.S. Commemorative Coins
912 Bob Wallace Ave.
Huntsville, Alabama 35801
        or
P.O. Box 302
Huntington Beach, California 92648

Dues are $15 per year and include a quarterly newsletter.

Society of Paper Money Collectors
c/o Ronald Horstman
P.O. Box 6011
St. Louis, Missouri 63139

Dues are $20 per year and include the bi-monthly publication, *Paper Money.*

Standing Liberty Quarter Collectors Society
P.O. Box 14762
Albuquerque, New Mexico 87191

A recently formed specialty group that intends to issue a quarterly journal, *MacNeil's Notes.* Dues are $10 per year.

Token and Medal Society
P.O. Box 360
Blackwood, New Jersey 08012

A large active group that publishes the *TAMS Journal* and

conducts an annual banquet at the yearly ANA convention. Write for current dues information.

These are only a few of the rare coin and currency publications, and some may be available at your local library. As mentioned earlier in this chapter, another superb resource is the American Numismatic Association (ANA) library. The ANA is the world's largest organization for collectors of coins, medals, tokens, paper money and other numismatic items, and members range in age from youngsters to seniors. ANA members can borrow from over 30,000 different reference items without charge, except for postage and insurance. It is one of the excellent reasons to join the ANA. Members receive the monthly magazine *The Numismatist*, and there are many other benefits of being a member.

The ANA's educational services department has developed a correspondence course written by some of the best known, most respected numismatic authorities in the United States including Walter Breen, Kenneth Bressett, Alan Herbert, Robert W. Julian, Eric Newman, and Anthony Swiatek.

For a membership brochure and information about the revised (1990) correspondence course, you can call the ANA's toll-free phone number, 800-367-9723 (in Colorado, 719-632-2646), or write to the ANA at 818 North Cascade Ave., Colorado Springs, Colorado 80903.

Now that you've read the experts' recommendations and my suggestions on additional reading materials, there is only one remaining piece of coin collecting advice to remember: HAVE FUN! Then tell a friend about numismatics.

About the Author

DONN PEARLMAN is an award-winning Chicago broadcaster who has been collecting coins since the age of eight with time out as an adolescent to spend money on other things. In 1989 he was elected to the Board of Governors of the American Numismatic Association. A member of more than a dozen local, regional, and national numismatic organizations from California to Florida, he has served on the Board of Directors of the Numismatic Literary Guild and is a past president of the Morton Grove, Illinois Coin Club.

In 1977, the Professional Numismatists Guild honored him as recipient of the prestigious "Sol Kaplan Award for Outstanding Service to Numismatics" for investigative reporting of suspected over-grading practices by some mail-order coin dealers. Twice he has been an invited guest speaker at the Numismatic Symposium conferences in Sydney, Australia, and he actively is involved in the annual Chicago International Coin Fairs.

His monthly column, "Pearlman's People," appears in *The Numismatist*—the journal of the ANA, and his by-line frequently has appeared in many other hobby publications. Pearlman's previous books published by Bonus Books, Inc., are *Breaking into Broadcasting*, *Collecting Baseball Cards*, and *Making Money With Baseball Cards* (co-authored with Paul M. Green).